Physical Characteristics of the Manchester Terrier

(from The Kennel Club breed standard)

Body: Short with well sprung ribs, slightly arched over the loin and cut up behin

Hindquarters: Strong and muscular, well bent at stifle.

Tail: Short and set on where arch of back ends, thick where it joins body, tapering to a point.

Coat: Close, smooth and glossy, of firm texture.

Size: Ideal height at shoulder: Dogs 41 cm (16 inches); Bitches 38 cm (15 inches).

Feet: Small, semi-hare footed and strong with well arched toes.

Manchester Terrier

◇

By Muriel P Lee

Contents

Health Care of Your Manchester Terrier 97

Discover how to select a proper veterinary surgeon and care for your dog at all stages of life. Topics include vaccinations, skin problems, dealing with external and internal parasites and common medical and behavioural conditions.

Your Veteran Manchester Terrier 126

Consider the care of your veteran Manchester Terrier, including the proper diet for a veteran. Recognise the signs of an ageing dog, both behavioural and medical; implement a special-care programme with your veterinary surgeon and become comfortable with making the final decisions and arrangements for your veteran Manchester Terrier.

Showing Your Manchester Terrier 133

Experience the conformation dog show world and other types of canine competition. Learn about The Kennel Club, the different types of shows and the making of a champion. Also learn about the FCI, the world's international kennel club.

Behaviour of Your Manchester Terrier 140

Learn to recognise and handle common behavioural problems in your Manchester Terrier, including barking, jumping up, aggression with people and other dogs, chewing, digging and more.

PUBLISHED IN THE UNITED KINGDOM BY:

INTERPET
PUBLISHING

Vincent Lane, Dorking, Surrey RH4 3YX England

ISBN 1-84286-056-9

Photography by Michael Trafford, with additional photographs by:

Norvia Behling, TJ Calhoun, Carolina Biological Supply, Doskocil, Isabelle Francais, James Hayden-Yoav, James R Hayden, RBP, Carol Ann Johnson, Bill Jonas, Dwight R Kuhn, Dr Dennis Kunkel, Mikki Pet Products, Phototake, Jean Claude Revy, Dr Andrew Spielman and Alice van Kempen.

Illustrations by Patricia Peters.

The publisher would like to thank all of the owners of the Manchester Terriers featured in this book, including Nerolie de Lavis-Trafford.

Originally known as the Black and Tan Terrier, the Manchester Terrier is believed to be the oldest of the terrier breeds and the progenitor of many other related breeds.

BLACK AND TANS IN OILS

The Manchester Terrier has been a popular subject for painting over the years. Sydenham Edwards included a Black and Tan Terrier in a painting produced in 1800; B A Hyland depicted a perky, smart Toy Manchester in an early painting; John Paul painted 'The Pug Pearl' and 'The Manchester Terrier Beauty' in 1871; in 1830 'Two Dogs in a Landscape' shows a small Manchester Terrier squaring off against a much larger dog. George Pai painted a favourite pet Manchester for his client with the dog wearing a lovely coat and probably ready for a walk with his master. Well-known artist Arthur Wardle's 'English Toy Terriers' shows a trio of very small Manchesters.

Originally the Manchester Terrier was called the Black and Tan Terrier in its land of origin: England, of course, where over 90% of the terrier breeds began. The terrier, from the Latin word *terra*, meaning earth, is a dog that has been bred to work beneath the ground to drive out small and large vermin, rodents and other animals that can be a nuisance to rural life.

Many of the terrier breeds were derived from a similar ancestor and, as recently as the mid-1800s, the terriers fell roughly into two basic categories: the rough-coated, short-legged dogs, which tended to come from Scotland; and the longer legged, smooth-coated dogs, which were bred in England. The terriers, although they may differ in type, all have the same character, being game dogs that go after vermin and who also make good companions for their masters.

As early as 1735, *The Sportsman's Dictionary* described the terrier as 'as a kind of hound, used only or chiefly for hunting the fox or badger. He creeps into the ground and then nips and bites the fox and badger, either by tearing them in pieces with his teeth, or else hauling them and pulling them by force out of their lurking holes.' The dogs were bred to go to ground with courage and conviction. Those who were unable to do the job were destroyed and those who could do the proper work were bred to one another with little regard for type. The Manchester Terrier, it must be noted, is not a digging terrier but rather a dog to cope with vermin on the docks and ships, where its contribution during the Industrial Revolution in England was very significant.

Most of the terrier backgrounds are obscure but, fortunately for us, the Manchester Terrier's history is more straightforward, and older, than many of the terrier breeds. The Manchester Terrier is probably the oldest of all terrier breeds, having been mentioned in the first of the canine breed books written in 1570. Authors and Manchester breeders Nerolie de Lavis-Trafford and Margaret

EAR CROPPING

Ear cropping consists of surgically trimming the ear leathers and then training the ears to stand upright. Originally, cropping was done to prevent the ears from being bitten by any adversary. With fighting dogs and terriers, cropped ears gave the opponent less to hang on to. Ear cropping also was considered important for cosmetic purposes, as it gives the dog a very smart look. Fortunately, today the tradition of cropping ears has been banned in the UK, and dogs with cropped ears cannot be shown. Dogs can be shown in the United States with either cropped or uncropped ears, but, in certain breeds, cropped ears are a requirement for showing in America.

Clowes suggest that the Manchester and the Welsh Terrier share a like ancestor. This is an excellent theory and one that most cynologists support. History sometimes leaves a trace or a 'thumbprint' for us to follow, as is the case with the Manchester and the Welsh Terriers. The classic 'thumbprints' on the Manchester develop as the dog matures, whereas the Welsh may be born with 'thumbprints,' which disappear in due course.

The Black and Tan, as it was then called, was a heavier dog and less known for his graceful looks than today's dog. Even so, he was a fearless dog with great speed and he could clean a barn of rats in very short order. Through the generations, he developed into a more delicate and graceful animal. It has been said that the old Black and Tan was unsurpassed in his ratting abilities. In the early years, the dog's ability to kill many rats in a short period of time was much more highly regarded than the actual look of the dog itself.

Breed scholars cite a smooth-coated Black and Tan Terrier as early as 1790, likely the earliest reference being in *A History of Quadrupeds*, written by avian artist and wood engraver, Thomas Bewick (1753–1828). Bewick notes that the smooth-coated terriers, sometimes 'black

Black and Tan a more refined body, a finer skull, a thinner and smoother coat, a longer muzzle and an arched loin. Overall, the Whippet added the class and style to the Manchester while maintaining the speed and rat-killing skills of the Black and Tan. In addition to the Whippet, it is thought that the Greyhound

OLD BLACKS AND OLD WHITES

A Croxton Smith notes in his book *About Our Dogs* that in the mid-1800s the dog was sometimes referred to as an English Terrier. 'In the present dog, our English Terrier must be either a Black and Tan and then it is called the Manchester Terrier or pure white. The latter, preferred by only a few, was called the English Terrier. Eventually this very handsome dog died out whereas the Manchester continues to be bred, shown and loved as a house pet.'

The Welsh Terrier, some believe, shares a similar ancestor with the Manchester Terrier.

with tanned legs,' was 'inferior in size, strength and hardiness.'

Manchester, located in the northwest of the country, was a well-known centre for two popular poor men's sports: rat killing and rabbit coursing. In addition, these activities gave the spectator ample opportunity to place bets on the better animal. John Hulme, in the early 1800s, thought that by crossing a Whippet with the Black and Tan, he could breed a dog that could be used in both sports. The crossing to the Whippet gave the

The English Toy Terrier, the small version of the Manchester Terrier, is a separate breed in the UK, though in America it is called the Toy Manchester Terrier, a variety of the Manchester Terrier. The American toy dogs are lower on leg, generally smaller and with less reach of neck.

and Italian Greyhound were also introduced into the breeding programmes.

It is interesting to note at this point that the Manchester Terrier has contributed its genes to a number of breeds as well, at least one of which enjoys tremendous popularity around the world. The Dobermann and Jagdterrier of Germany, the Beauceron of France, our own Lancashire Heeler and also the Australian Cattle Dog are counted among the breeds who have Manchester blood flowing in their 'blue' veins.

By the mid-1800s the Black and Tan's name was changed to the Manchester Terrier. Although the breed was found throughout

England, there was a prominence of the breed in the town after which it was named. James Watson writes in 1905 in *The Dog Book*, 'The first English stud book contains the entry of 102 Black and Tan Terriers, other than toys, of this number we can, without any reference for

14.3 RATS PER MINUTE

In 1889 a rat-baiting contest was held in Antwerp, Belgium, with large and vicious rats that came from the sewers of Paris. The Black and Tan proved the winner of all of the terriers that were entered, killing more rats, more quickly, than any other breed. Jacko, a Black and Tan owned by Mr Shaw, killed 100 rats in 7 minutes.

further information, but solely from our recollections of where many of the exhibitors and breeders resided, pick out no less than 52 hailing from Manchester or its immediate neighbourhood, or bred there.' Mr Watson wanted to discourage any further discussion that the dog was incorrectly named. The name change was supported by many in the fancy, not the least was Mr Henry Lacy from Yorkshire. Lacy was one of the great dogmen of his day, influential and well connected. His dog, Belcher, was considered the best Manchester of the time.

As the Manchesters were bred, litters contained pups of normal size plus a few of diminutive size. Breeders found that the small Manchesters were in high demand by the puppy-buying public, especially the buyers in London, and a few started breeding the smaller puppy of one litter to the smallest puppy of another litter, thus breeding the English Toy Terrier. Soon dogs were bred as tiny as 2 to 3 pounds and the Toys lost substance and vigour. Breeders began to realise that they were not producing the dog of their desires. Reality took hold and once again breeders bred healthy dogs of substance with a return to type and soundness.

By the 1870s, the breed reached its peak of popularity and one of the more known breeders of the time was Mr Sam Handley of Manchester. He bred a number of good dogs and did much to popularise the breed. As the breed became popular among the gentry, it was also called "The Gentleman's Terrier."

In 1909, England banned ear cropping and the breed started to

Manchester breeders are a devoted and hardy lot, having stuck by our breed through two difficult World Wars and the looming threat of extinction.

struggle to survive. With the advent of World War I, breeding of all dogs was greatly curtailed. Travel was restricted, dog shows were suspended and it was difficult for individuals to feed themselves let alone a kennel of dogs. The breed suffered dramatically and only because of a few individuals, Colonel Dean, Miss Hopwood and Mr Hazelwood,

A MATTER OF CROPPING

When ears were no longer allowed to be cropped in England, many of the older breeders became discouraged and quit breeding the Manchester Terrier. In England, the breed is now bred with either an attractive button ear or an upright ear whereas in America only the Standard Manchester can have cropped ears. Toys may have the natural button or upright ears as cropped ears are a disqualification.

did the breed survive at all.

In the 1920s, Manchesters began to revive and slowly registration numbers began to increase. In 1924, The Kennel Club officially approved the name Manchester Terrier, and the British Manchester Terrier Club was formed in 1937 with its first meeting held, fittingly, at the Manchester Championship Show. As the breed appeared to be recovering, World War II broke out and this time the breed suffered extensively and was on the brink of extinction.

The efforts of Mr William Ward of the Livesey kennel must be noted, as he was responsible for working diligently on improving and cementing type in the breed. His kennel, located in Blackburn, produced many top winners and producers, many of which can be seen in pedigrees to this day. A long-time Manchester breeder from the 1900s was Mr Anstey, whose dogs and spin-off prefixes were a force to behold for decades in England. Anstey's most famous dog was Prince Rufus, who remained unbeaten in Championship Shows for many years, having accumulated a breed-record 17 Challenge Certificates. Prince Rufus's offspring, Ch Red Monarch of Dreams, was a key dog in the breed's history, the 'Of Dreams' prefix belonging to Miss

Schwabe. Red Monarch is credited for keeping the breed going in England after World War II, by producing a litter of two with Julie of Dreams at the age of 13. Pretty Kitten of Dreams and Red Robin of Dreams, the two dogs produced in the litter, were bred along with Oldlane Dagger, another older dog, and Branlys Scaramouche, an American import of significance!

In 1946, only 11 dogs were known to exist in England. The breed started to revive when The Kennel Club licenced controlled interbreeding with the English Toy Terrier (formerly known simply as the Miniature Manchester Terrier; in the US, the smaller dogs are called Toy Manchester Terriers and appear stockier than the English Toy Terriers, which are generally taller, leggier with greater reach of neck). In addition, the US imports of Sir Oscar of Chatham Farms and Gwinney Willows Thunderstorm added much-needed new blood to the breed. In 1955, the first post-war champion was made up, Oldlane Sensation, owned by Mr W Hardwick. Scottish showman, Mr K Cassels, a long-time Manchester advocate, acquired some Oldlane dogs, most of which had impressive pedigrees. These dogs, including Sorisdale Asphodel and Oldlane Comeback, enjoyed popularity in the mid-1950s, when the breed was very much in good hands.

Mr Richard and Mrs E E Knight entered the Manchester world in the 1950s, with their import of Sir Oscar of Chatham Farms and Gwinny Willows Thunderstorm from the US. Although these two dogs were disqualified from exhibition in Kennel Club shows, due to their cropped ears, they were used extensively for breeding and can be found in nearly every British pedigree of the present day. The Eaglespur prefix of Mrs Knight (currently Mrs Teague Knight) produced such dogs as Ch Eaglespur Articstarre, Ch Eaglespur Lancehead, Ch Eagle Spur Black Prince at Manterr and Ch Eaglespur Lord Pegasus. This kennel is a great credit to the breed and has continued to thrive for many years.

Miss Phil Margiotta and her Prioryhill prefix must be counted among the celebrated Manchesters of the current day. Top dog Ch Prioryhill Baronet did considerable winning and appears in many pedigrees today, as have many of the lovely Prioryhill bitches. Mr Brian Moorhouse began his Manterr prefix, doing considerable winning at the shows. Later, in conjunction with Mrs de Forest Keys and her Keyline dogs, Moorhouse produced an impressive string of champions.

Dobermann.

THE BLACK AND TAN FAMILY OF DOGS

The old Black and Tan Terrier lives on in many breeds today beyond the Manchester Terrier. Among the other breeds that share the black and tan coloration are: the Miniature Pinscher, the Dobermann, the German Pinscher, the Bloodhound, the Dachshund, the Lancashire Heeler, the Beauceron and the Austrian Shorthaired Pinscher. This group of dogs breeds true to colour with the solid black predominating and dark tan markings.

Miniature Pinscher.

MANCHESTERS IN AMERICA

Manchesters were exported to the US and Canada in the late 1800s. The first Manchester registered in the US was Lever, son of Ch Voltigern, who was bred in England and exported in 1887 when he was a year of age. Alf George imported a bitch called Nettle who was considered a quality bitch even though she had a very limited pedigree. James Watson, who has written extensively about the early Manchesters in the US, notes the efforts taken to help popularise the breed: 'The only thing that induced the club to have Dr Stables judge was his offer to judge in Highland costume. This, Secretary Tileston, thought would be an immense advertising card and the cost of importing the judge was incurred for that purpose alone. When he arrived minus the promised costume there was a good deal of disappointment.'

An early breeder and exhibitor of the breed was Mr Edward Lever of Philadelphia. Later, Dr H T Foote came along and, with dedication and persistence, he bred and exhibited Manchesters for a good 20 years until his wife took a fancy to the Scottish Terrier and he followed her into the new breed. The breed in America fell upon hard times after Dr Foote transferred his allegiances to the Scottie.

Few Manchesters were registered with the American Kennel Club, but some breeders did keep breeding even though they didn't register their dogs.

A small group of dedicated breeders wanted to revive the popularity of the breed and in 1923 the Manchester Terrier Club of America was formed. Although the Toy Manchester Terrier continued to maintain some popularity over the years, the Standard declined in popularity and, by 1952, the Manchester Terrier Club of America was without breed representation. With thanks to the American Toy Manchester Terrier Club, the proposal was submitted to the American Kennel Club (AKC) that the two varieties (Standard and Toy) be recognised as one breed. The American Toy Manchester Terrier Club changed its name to the American Manchester Terrier Club and became the parent club for both the Standard and Toy varieties.

In the 1960s, American breeder Myrtle Klensch, a handler, fell in love with the Manchester Terrier and started breeding under the Salutaire prefix. She put the first Best in Show on a Standard Manchester, Am Ch R-Way Morning Glory, bred by Kathy Tandazzoi. She followed this with a Best in Show on her homebred Ch Salutaire Word to the Wise, who won many all-breed Bests in Show. Another noteworthy Salutaire Manchester was Am Ch Salutaire Sweet Talkin' Man CD, bred by M Klensch and C Ross and owned by P Dresser. This offspring of Am Ch Salutaire Word to the Wise won Westminster Kennel Club Best of Breed five times (1991–1994 and 1996), among some 500 Bests of Breed, as well as about 10 Bests in Show. Myrtle was a tireless supporter of the breed and the first to understand the value of genetic testing for problems within the breed. She served as president of the Manchester Terrier Club of America and during that time the club voted to move the national specialities around the country rather than holding them only on the East Coast. This helped the breed to be seen and known throughout the country. She was a tireless campaigner of her dogs and the breed, and it was a great loss to the breed and the whole dog fancy when she died in August 2000.

In both England and the United States, the Manchester Terrier remains in good hands with their national breed clubs and a dedicated group of breeders. Although there has never been a great demand for puppies, the breed is healthy and maintains a fairly high recognition rate in both countries.

CHARACTERISTICS OF THE

MANCHESTER TERRIER

The Manchester Terrier is a small, confident, alert and agile dog whose origins trace as far back as mediaeval England. This is an intelligent terrier with a smart, keen look about him. With his great speed and agility, he was originally bred to rout out the rats in the barns and the waterways. He has evolved into a most pleasant household companion, being of a nice size to fit into either a country house or a city flat. He possesses personality-plus and is an active dog. Unlike other terriers, many which require substantial grooming, the Manchester is an easy keeper, requiring little more than a weekly brushing and a wipe-down with a damp cloth.

Some terriers, like the Manchester, are 'below the knee' in size, but in spite of their size, all terriers are masculine dogs and do not show any sign of timidity or shyness. These are busy dogs, on their toes and ready for action! If you are looking for a sedentary lap dog, this will not be the breed for you.

The Manchester has a very steady disposition and fits in well with family life, whether it be in a large country house or a small flat in the city. He may be wary of strangers but will accept them once he has had a chance to look them over. He's a cocky dog who may not go out and start a fight but will surely stand his ground when challenged. This is not a dog that will lie about the house trying to keep his master or mistress happy. He has been bred as a hunter, a dog to go after vermin, and he can be ready to work at the 'drop of a rat.' Unlike the 'go to ground' terriers, the Manchester is not a digger, as evidenced by his semi-hare feet (not round for digging) and his slightly sloping fetlocks (not short and straight). He has been described as extremely clean, alert, bright and handsome, all descriptives that he lives up to. He is quickly house-trained, unlike some other terriers. He is charming and sensitive, expressive and inquisitive. He is well mannered and 'truly an asset to the most discerning companion.' He has a sparkling personality, a keen sense of smell, excellent hearing and amazing agility. In 1935, the AKC described the

Manchesters enjoy the company of well-behaved children. This breed will accept as much exercise as you are willing to provide, but they are not as active as many of the other terrier breeds.

Manchester Terrier as such: 'He is still *per se* a vermin dog, unequalled and is capable of doling his own in a rough-and-tumble scrap with anything living, and will tackle anything his weight or twice his size.'

Common characteristics for all terriers are their desire to work with great enthusiasm and courage. They all have large and powerful teeth for the size of their bodies; they have keen hearing and excellent eyesight no matter how many generations they have been bred as pets, and the purpose for which the breed was bred will always remain with the dog.

The Manchester Terrier is a versatile dog and a reliable house dog and companion. If you like to work with your dog, you will find the Manchester to be a happy and willing participant in whatever area you choose, be it obedience work, agility, trailing, therapy or flyball. This is a smart little dog that likes to please, to keep busy and to be challenged. Give him any job that requires a bit of brain activity on his part and he will be content and productive.

And once a Manchester has

learned his tricks, they will not be forgotten! Of course, because of his intelligence, it is best to establish very early on who is the head of the household, and the very basics in obedience lessons are always a good idea. A word of caution to those with small children: Because the Manchester is a fairly small dog, young children must be taught very early that this is not a dog to be pulled around, sat upon or, in general, handled roughly. Children must treat their (and all) dogs with respect.

If you are a first-time dog owner, you must be aware of your responsibility toward your new friend. Either keep your dog on a leash or in your fenced garden. Your Manchester, if loose and trotting along at your side, will spot a squirrel across a busy street. His instincts will react quickly and he will dart across the street, never minding the traffic. Therefore, some rudimentary obedience training should be in line so your chum will sit when asked to, come when called and, in general, act like a little gentleman.

Manchesters, as with other terriers, can be a challenge in the obedience ring. Terriers are not easy breeds to work with in obedience as, with their intelligence and independent spirit, they can sometimes be more trying to train than had been anticipated. You will see Golden Retrievers, Poodles and Miniature Schnauzers in abundance in obedience classes as these are breeds that are easy to work with. Not only are they intelligent but, more importantly, they have a willingness to please their master. However, once a Manchester learns his lessons, he will never forget them. The terrier is easily distracted and busy but he is an intelligent dog and he does respond to training. Of course, when training a smart and independent dog, the handler will

Blest with intelligence and an independent spirit, the Manchester Terrier is the choice of a discerning dog owner.

When not acting like little gentlemen, Manchesters enjoy running amok, for the fun of it or for the sake of catching an ill-fated rodent. These puppies are having a grand time in some fresh sawdust.

often learn humility while the dog is learning his heels and downs. The Manchester is a quick, alert and intelligent dog, and he likes his owner to be his equal.

HEALTH CONSIDERATIONS

Overall, the well-bred Manchester is a healthy dog and most problems that may come up can be avoided by good breeding and adequate care in raising the dog. However, there are a few problems that are known in the breed, and you would be wise to ask the breeder of the dog that you are purchasing if he has had his dogs tested for von Willibrand's disease, a blood disorder. VWD is the most common bleeding disorder of man and dogs and affects many breeds. This is an inherited disease and Manchesters can be either free of VWD, carriers of the gene or "bleeders." Reputable breeders have their dogs' blood tested to make certain that they are not breeding affected dogs.

Skin disorders such as infections and irritations can also be a problem and, if you detect problems of this type, you should contact your veterinary surgeon for assistance. The aforementioned problems do exist in the breed and a buyer should be aware of them. Do not be turned away from the breed but do be aware that if the breeder of your puppy is reputable and aware of these problems, he will be doing his utmost to keep them out of his line.

MANCHESTER TERRIER

Compact, elegant and sound well sums up the ideal Manchester Terrier. Abide by the standard to select a typical, well-bred Manchester Terrier, whether you are pursuing a career in the show ring or just a handsome pet dog.

Each breed approved by The Kennel Club has a standard that provides a mental picture of what the specific breed should look like. All reputable breeders strive to produce animals that will meet the requirements of the standard. Many breeds were developed for a specific purpose, e.g. retrieving, going to ground, guarding or hunting. In addition to having dogs that look like proper Manchester Terriers, the standard assures that the dogs will have the personality, movement and intelligence that are sought after in the breed.

Standards were originally written by experts who had a love and a concern for the breed. They knew that the essential character-

MARKINGS

Clarity and depth of colour are desirable in the short-coated black dog with tan points. The aim of the breeders is like breeding a thoroughbred race horse. Note in the 'Colour' section of the standard that there are very specific markings for the Manchester. Notably, there is tan pencilling on the toes up the inside of the legs, pencilling on the toes up the inside of the legs and 'rosettes' on each side of the chest above the front legs. Likewise, the 'thumbprint' and tan vent are of similar importance.

istics of the Manchester Terrier were unlike those of any other breed and that care must be taken that these characteristics were maintained through the generations. As time progressed and breeders became more aware that certain areas of the dog needed better descriptions or more definition, breeders would meet together and develop a more elaborate, detailed standard. However, standards for any breed are never changed on a whim, and serious study and exchange between breeders takes place before any move is made.

THE KENNEL CLUB BREED STANDARD FOR THE MANCHESTER TERRIER

General Appearance: Compact, elegant and sound with substance.

Characteristics: Keen, alert, gay and sporting.

Temperament: Discerning and devoted.

Head and Skull: Long skull, flat and narrow, level and wedge shaped without showing cheek muscles, well filled up under eyes, with tapering, tight lipped mouth.

Eyes: Small, dark and sparkling. Almond shaped, not prominent.

Ears: Small and 'V' shaped, carried well above topline of head

and hanging close to head above eyes.

Mouth: Jaws level with perfect scissor bite (i.e. upper teeth closely overlapping lower teeth and set square to jaws).

Neck: Fairly long and tapering from shoulder to head, slightly arched at crest, free from throatiness.

Forequarters: Shoulders clean and well sloped. Front narrow and deep. Forelegs quite straight, set on well under dog and of proportionate length to body.

Body: Short with well sprung ribs, slightly arched over the loin and cut up behind ribs.

Hindquarters: Strong and muscular, well bent at stifle. Hind legs neither cow hocked nor with feet turned in.

The skull should be long, flat and narrow, well filled in under the eyes and wedge-shaped. This Manchester has an excellent headpiece.

POUND EXCHANGE UK/US

In the UK, the Manchester should weight about 7.25 kg (16 pounds). The smaller breed in the Toy Group is called the English Toy Terrier. In America, the Manchester Terrier standard states that the weight for the breed is over 12 pounds and not exceeding 22 pounds. The Toy Manchester Terrier, which is classified in the Toy Group, weighs 12 pounds and under.

Above left: An ideal head of a Manchester Terrier with natural button ears, showing correct type and proportion. Below right: An ideal Manchester Terrier in profile. This dog has button ears and shows correct type, balance and substance.

Feet: Small, semi-hare footed and strong with well arched toes.

Tail: Short and set on where arch of back ends, thick where it joins body, tapering to a point, carried not higher than level of back.

Gait/Movement: Straight, free and balanced with good reach in forequarters and driving power behind.

Coat: Close, smooth and glossy, of firm texture.

Colour: Jet black and rich mahogany tan, distributed as follows: on head; muzzle tanned to nose, nose and nasal bone jet black. Small tan spot on each cheek and above each eye, under jaw and throat tanned with distinct tanned 'V.' Legs from knee downward tanned, with the exception of toes, which shall be pencilled with black, and a distinct mark (thumb mark) immediately above feet. Inside hind legs tanned but divided with black at stifle joint. Under tail

BREEDER'S BLUEPRINT

If you are considering breeding your bitch, it is very important that you are familiar with the breed standard. Reputable breeders breed with the intention of producing dogs that are as close as possible to the standard and that contribute to the advancement of the breed. Study the standard for both physical appearance and temperament, and make certain your bitch and your chosen stud dog measure up.

tanned, vent tanned by marking as narrow as possible so that it is covered by tail. A slight tan mark on each side of chest. Tan on outside hind legs, commonly called breeching is undesirable. In all cases black should not run into tan and vice versa, but division between colours clearly defined.

Size: Ideal height at shoulder: Dogs 41 cm (16 inches); Bitches 38 cm (15 inches).

Faults: Any departure from the foregoing points should be considered a fault and the seriousness with which the fault should be regarded should be in exact proportion to its degree.

Note: Male animals should have two apparently normal testicles fully descended into the scrotum.

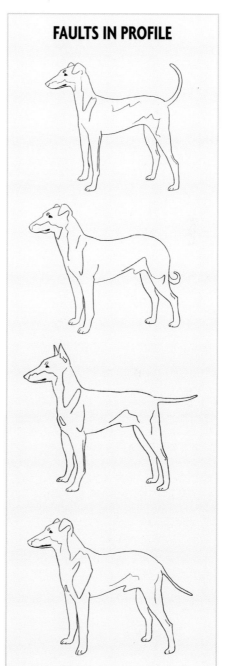

FAULTS IN PROFILE

Generally lacking substance and bone, shallow chested, high in rear with dip in topline, gay tail, upright shoulders.

Short, coarse head, upright shoulders, soft topline, high in the rear, ring at end of tail.

Dog with cropped ears showing ewe-neck, upright shoulders, weak pasterns, flat feet and lack of adequate angulation in the rear.

Short, thick neck, loaded shoulders, toes out in front, excessive arch over loin, weak rear lacking angulation and power.

MANCHESTER TERRIER

WHERE TO BEGIN

The Manchester Terrier certainly has many marvellous qualities that attract new owners to the breed all of the time. Beyond the breed's versatility, convenient size, easy-care attributes and intelligence, the breed is one of the most charming and amusing chums you could have around your home. If you are convinced that the Manchester Terrier is

BOY OR GIRL?

An important consideration to be discussed is the sex of your puppy. For a family companion, a bitch may be the better choice, considering the female's inbred concern for all young creatures and her accompanying tolerance and patience. It is always advisable to spay a pet bitch, which may guarantee her a longer life.

When visiting a litter, spend some time getting to know the puppies. A game of 'follow the stick' can indicate which of the pups is the leader and which is the lagger.

A breeder should radiate with pride and love for every puppy she sells. When you find a breeder who smiles and sheds a tear as you take your new charge home, you will know that you have selected a winner.

the ideal dog for you, it's time to learn about where to find a puppy and what to look for. Locating a litter of Manchester Terriers will not be as simple as finding a local litter of Border Collies or Labradors, but this is not necessarily a drawback. In popular breeds like those two illustrious ones mentioned, potential owners deal with an onslaught of irresponsible breeders, profit-minded sellers who have little or no regard for

PREPARING FOR PUP

Unfortunately, when a puppy is bought by someone who does not take into consideration the time and attention that dog ownership requires, it is the puppy who suffers when he is either abandoned or placed in a shelter by a frustrated owner. So all of the 'homework' you do in preparation for your pup's arrival will benefit you both. The more informed you are, the more you will know what to expect and the better equipped you will be to handle the ups and downs of raising a puppy. Hopefully, everyone in the household is willing to do his part in raising and caring for the pup. The anticipation of owning a dog often brings a lot of promises from excited family members: 'I will walk him every day,' 'I will feed him,' 'I will housetrain him,' etc., but these things take time and effort, and promises can be forgotten easily once the novelty of the new pet has worn off.

Every member of the family should participate in the selection process. Keep in mind that children must be instructed as to how to handle a Manchester puppy properly.

the overall good of the breed. Manchester breeders—a select group to be sure!—are a most discriminate band of professionals who breed for the betterment of this brilliant breed and not for financial gain. (That's not to say that there isn't one or two bad apples in the whole UK…there's always a chance!) Nevertheless, a potential owner should contact The Kennel Club or the British Manchester Terrier Club for a list of breeders in your region or county.

An established breeder will sell you a puppy at a fair price if, and only if, the breeder determines that you are a suitable, worthy owner of his dogs. These breeders should be established

with a number of years' experience in Manchester Terriers, and dogs in general. Many of these folk have been 'in dogs' for 20 or more years. Such an established breeder can be relied upon for advice, no matter what time of day or night. A reputable breeder will accept a puppy back, without questions, should you decide that this is not the right dog for you.

When choosing a breeder, reputation is much more important than convenience of location. Given the relative rarity of the breed, you may have to travel some distance to acquire your Manchester, but it will be worth the day's journey.

Potential owners are encouraged to attend dog shows (or trials) to see the Manchester Terriers in action, to meet the owners and handlers firsthand

HANDLE WITH CARE

You should be extremely careful about handling tiny puppies. Not that you might hurt them, but that the pups' mother may exhibit what is called 'maternal aggression.' It is a natural, instinctive reaction for the dam to protect her young against anything she interprets as predatory or possibly harmful to her pups. The sweetest, most gentle of bitches, after whelping a litter, often reacts this way, even to her owner.

and to get an idea of what Manchester Terriers look like outside a photographer's lens. Provided you approach the handlers when they are not busy with the dogs, most are more than willing to answer questions, recommend breeders and give advice.

Now that you have contacted and met a breeder or two and made your choice about which breeder is best suited to your needs, it's time to visit the litter. Keep in mind that many breeders have waiting lists. Sometimes new owners have to wait as long as two years for a puppy. If you are really committed to the breeder whom you've selected, then you will wait (and hope for an early arrival!). If not, you may have to go with your second-choice breeder, though you likely will not have to wait for more than a 'season' or two.

When choosing your Manchester Terrier, you simply should select a pup that is friendly and attractive. Manchester Terriers generally have small litters, averaging four or five puppies, so selection is limited once you have located a desirable litter. Beware of the shy or overly aggressive puppy; be especially conscious of the nervous Manchester Terrier pup. Don't let sentiment or emotion trap you into buying the runt of the litter.

The gender of your puppy is largely a matter of personal taste, although male Manchester Terriers are slightly larger and usually more aggressive than their bitch counterparts.

Breeders commonly allow visitors to see the litter by around the fifth or sixth week, and puppies leave for their new homes between the eighth and

PUPPY APPEARANCE
Your puppy should have a well-fed appearance but not a distended abdomen, which may indicate worms or incorrect feeding, or both. The body should be firm, with a solid feel. The skin of the abdomen should be pale pink and clean, without signs of scratching or rash. Check the hind legs to make certain that dewclaws were removed, if any were present at birth.

Take your time in selecting your puppy. You want an alert and energetic puppy who looks and acts healthy and sound.

tenth week. Puppies need to learn the rules of the pack from their dam, and most dams continue teaching the pups manners and dos and don'ts until around the eighth week. Breeders spend significant amounts of time with the Manchester Terrier toddlers so that they are able to interact with the 'other species,' i.e. humans. Given the long history that dogs and humans have, bonding between the two species is natural but must be nurtured. A well-bred, well-socialised Manchester Terrier pup wants nothing more than to be near you.

Always check the bite of your selected puppy to be sure that it is neither overshot nor undershot. This may not be too noticeable on a young puppy but it is a fairly common problem with certain lines of Manchester Terriers.

COMMITMENT OF OWNERSHIP

After considering all of these factors, you have most likely already made some very important decisions about selecting your puppy. You have chosen a Manchester Terrier, which means that you have decided which characteristics you want in a dog and what type of dog will best fit into your family and lifestyle. If you have selected a breeder, you have gone a step further—you have done your research and found a responsible, conscientious person who breeds quality Manchester Terriers and who should be a reliable source of help as you and your puppy adjust to life together. If you have observed a litter in action, you have obtained a firsthand look at the dynamics of a puppy pack and, thus, you should have learned about each pup's individual personality—perhaps you have even found one that particularly appeals to you.

However, even if you have not yet found the Manchester

HEALTH FIRST
You should not even think about buying a puppy that looks sick, undernourished, overly frightened or nervous. Sometimes a timid puppy will warm up to you after a 30-minute 'let's-get-acquainted' session.

Terrier puppy of your dreams, observing pups will help you learn to recognise certain behaviour and to determine what a pup's behaviour indicates about his temperament. You will be able to pick out which pups are the leaders, which ones are less outgoing, confident, shy, playful, friendly, aggressive, etc. Equally as important, you will learn to recognise what an healthy pup should look and act like. All of these things will help you in your search, and when you find the Manchester Terrier that was meant for you, you will know it!

Researching your breed, selecting a responsible breeder and observing as many pups as possible are all important steps on the way to dog ownership. It may seem like a lot of effort… and you have not even taken the pup home yet! Remember, though, you cannot be too careful when it comes to deciding on the type of dog you want and finding out about your prospective pup's background. Buying a puppy is *not*—or should not be—just another whimsical purchase. This is one instance in which you actually do get to choose your own family!

PREPARING PUPPY'S PLACE IN YOUR HOME

Researching your breed and finding a breeder are only two aspects of the 'homework' you will have to do before taking your Manchester Terrier puppy home. You will also have to prepare your home and family for the new addition. Much as you would prepare a nursery for a newborn baby, you will need to designate a place in your

YOUR SCHEDULE . . .
If you lead an erratic, unpredictable life, with daily or weekly changes in your work requirements, consider the problems of owning a dog. The new puppy has to be fed regularly, socialised (loved, petted, handled, introduced to other people) and, most importantly, allowed to visit outdoors for toilet training. As the dog gets older, he can be more tolerant of deviations in its feeding and toilet relief.

PUPPY SELECTION

Your selection of a good puppy can be determined by your needs. A show potential or a good pet? It is your choice. Every puppy, however, should be of good temperament. Although show-quality puppies are bred and raised with emphasis on physical conformation, responsible breeders strive for equally good temperament. Do not buy from a breeder who concentrates solely on physical beauty at the expense of personality.

bringing him into what will become his home as well. Obviously, you did not buy a puppy so that he could take over your house, but in order for a puppy to grow into a stable, well-adjusted dog, he has to feel comfortable in his surroundings. Remember, he is leaving the warmth and security of his dam and littermates, as well as the familiarity of the only place he has ever known, so it is important to make his transition as easy as possible. By preparing a place in your home for the puppy, you are making him feel as welcome as possible in a strange new place. It should not take him long to get used to it, but the sudden shock of being transplanted is somewhat traumatic for a young pup. Imagine how a small child would feel in the same situation—that is how your puppy must be feeling. It is up to you to reassure him and to let him know, 'Little chap, you are going to like it here!'

WHAT YOU SHOULD BUY

home that will be the puppy's own. How you prepare your home will depend on how much freedom the dog will be allowed. Whatever you decide, you must ensure that he has a place that he can 'call his own.'

When you bring your new puppy into your home, you are

CRATE

To someone unfamiliar with the use of crates in dog training, it may seem like punishment to shut a dog in a crate, but this is not the case at all. Although all breeders do not advocate crate training, more and more breeders and trainers are recommend-

'YOU BETTER SHOP AROUND!'
Finding a reputable breeder who sells healthy pups is very important, but make sure that the breeder you choose is not only someone you respect but also someone with whom you feel comfortable. Your breeder will be a resource long after you buy your puppy, and you must be able to call with reasonable questions without being made to feel like a pest! If you don't connect on a personal level, investigate some other breeders before making a final decision.

ing crates as preferred tools for show puppies as well as pet puppies. Crates are not cruel—crates have many humane and highly effective uses in dog care and training. For example, crate training is a very popular and very successful house-training method. A crate can keep your dog safe during travel and, perhaps most importantly, a crate provides your dog with a place of his own in your home. It serves as a 'doggie bedroom' of sorts—your Manchester Terrier can curl up in his crate when he wants to sleep or when he just needs a break. Many dogs sleep in their crates overnight. With soft bedding and his favourite toy, a crate becomes a cosy pseudo-den for

your dog. Like his ancestors, he too will seek out the comfort and retreat of a den—you just happen to be providing him with something a little more luxurious than what his early ancestors enjoyed.

As far as purchasing a crate, the type that you buy is up to you. It will most likely be one of the two most popular types: wire or fibreglass. There are advantages and disadvantages to each type. For example, a wire crate is more open, allowing the air to flow through and affording the dog a view of what is going on around him, while a fibre-glass crate is sturdier. Both can double as car-travel crates, providing protection for the dog.

Your Manchester Terrier puppy will take a couple of days to start to feel comfortable in his new home. Be patient and don't rush the process—your pup will come around in no time.

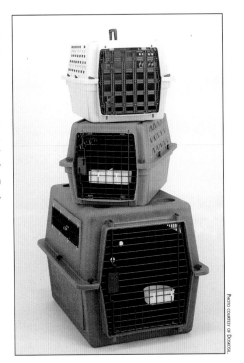

PHOTO COURTESY OF DOSKOCIL

twigs, etc., that the pup would use in the wild to make a den; the pup can make his own 'burrow' in the crate. Although your pup is far removed from his den-making ancestors, the denning instinct is still a part of his genetic makeup. Second, until you take your pup home, he has been sleeping amid the warmth of his dam and litter-mates, and while a blanket is not the same as a warm, breath-ing body, it still provides heat and something with which to snuggle. You will want to wash your pup's bedding frequently in case he has a toileting accident

The size of the crate is another thing to consider. Puppies do not stay puppies forever—in fact, sometimes it seems as if they grow right before your eyes. A medium-size crate is fine for a fully-grown Manchester Terrier, as you do not want the crate to be too large nor too small that the dog cannot stand up, lie down and turn around.

BEDDING

Veterinary bedding in the dog's crate will help the dog feel more at home and you may also like to pop in a small blanket. This will take the place of the leaves, in his crate, and replace or remove any bedding that becomes ragged and starts to fall apart.

Toys

Toys are a must for dogs of all ages, especially for curious playful pups. Puppies are the 'children' of the dog world, and what child does not love toys? Chew toys provide enjoyment for both dog and owner—your dog will enjoy playing with his favourite toys, while you will enjoy the fact that they distract him from your expensive shoes and leather sofa. Puppies love to

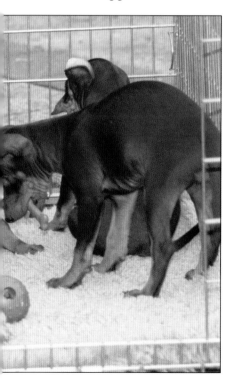

CRATE-TRAINING TIPS

During crate training, you should partition off the section of the crate in which the pup stays. If he is given too big an area, this will hinder your training efforts. Crate training is based on the fact that a dog does not like to soil his sleeping quarters, so it is ineffective to keep a pup in an area that is so big that he can eliminate in one end and get far enough away from it to sleep. Also, you want to make the crate den-like for the pup. Blankets and a favourite toy will make the crate cosy for the small pup; as he grows, you may want to evict some of his 'roommates' to make more room. It will take some coaxing at first, but be patient. Given some time to get used to it, your pup will adapt to his new home-within-a-home quite nicely.

Some breeders introduce the litter to a crate so that the puppies become accustomed to the enclosure. In time, each pup has his own crate in which to play and rest.

TOYS, TOYS, TOYS!

With a big variety of dog toys available, and so many that look like they would be a lot of fun for a dog, be careful in your selection. It is amazing what a set of puppy teeth can do to an innocent-looking toy, so, obviously, safety is a major consideration. Be sure to choose the most durable products that you can find. Hard nylon bones and toys are a safe bet, and many of them are offered in different scents and flavours that will be sure to capture your dog's attention. It is always fun to play a game of catch with your dog, and there are balls and flying discs that are specially made to withstand dog teeth.

chew; in fact, chewing is a physical need for pups as they are teething, and everything looks appetising! The full range of your possessions—from your favourite slipper to your new Oriental carpet—are fair game in the eyes of a teething pup. Puppies are not all that discerning when it comes to finding something to literally 'sink their teeth into'—everything tastes great!

Manchester Terrier puppies are fairly aggressive chewers and only the hardest, strongest toys should be offered to them. Breeders advise owners to resist stuffed toys, because they can become de-stuffed in no time. The overly excited pup may ingest the stuffing, which is neither digestible nor nutritious.

Similarly, squeaky toys are quite popular, but must be avoided for the Manchester Terrier. Perhaps a squeaky toy can be used as an aid in training, but not for free play. If a pup 'disembowels' one of these, the small plastic squeaker inside can be dangerous if swallowed. Monitor the condition of all your pup's toys carefully and get rid of any that have been chewed to the point of becoming potentially dangerous.

Be careful of natural bones, which have a tendency to splinter into sharp, dangerous pieces. Also be careful of rawhide, which can turn into pieces that are easy to swallow and become a mushy mess on your carpet.

LEAD

A nylon lead is probably the best option as it is the most resistant to puppy teeth should your pup take a liking to chewing on his lead. Of course, this is a habit that should be nipped in the bud, but if your pup likes to chew on his lead, he has a very slim chance of being able to chew through the strong nylon. Nylon leads are also lightweight, which is good for a young Manchester Terrier who is just getting used to the idea of walking on a lead. For everyday

Pet shops usually stock a wide selection of leads from which you may choose one suitable for your Manchester.

walking and safety purposes, the nylon lead is a good choice. As your pup grows up and gets used to walking on the lead, you may want to purchase a flexible lead. These leads allow you to extend the length to give the dog a broader area to explore or to shorten the length to keep the dog near you.

COLLAR

Your pup should get used to wearing a collar all the time since you will want to attach his ID tags to it. Plus, you have to attach the lead to something! A lightweight nylon collar is a good choice; make sure that it fits snugly enough so that the pup cannot wriggle out of it, but is loose enough so that it will not be uncomfortably tight around the pup's neck. You

FINANCIAL RESPONSIBILITY

Grooming tools, collars, leads, dog beds and, of course, toys will be expenses to you when you first obtain your pup, and the cost will continue throughout your dog's lifetime. If your puppy damages or destroys your possessions (as most puppies surely will!) or something belonging to a neighbour, you can calculate additional expense. There is also flea and pest control, which every dog owner faces more than once. You must be able to handle the financial responsibility of owning a dog.

The **BUCKLE COLLAR** is the standard collar used for everyday purposes. Be sure that you adjust the buckle on growing puppies. Check it every day. It can become too tight overnight! These collars can be made of leather or nylon. Attach your dog's identification tags to this collar.

The **CHOKE COLLAR** is constructed of highly polished steel so that it slides easily through the stainless steel loop. The idea is that the dog controls the pressure around his neck and he will stop pulling if the collar becomes uncomfortable. It should *never* be left on a dog when not training.

The **HALTER** is for a trained dog that has to be restrained to prevent running away, chasing a cat and the like. Considered the most humane of all collars, it is frequently used on smaller dogs on which collars are not comfortable.

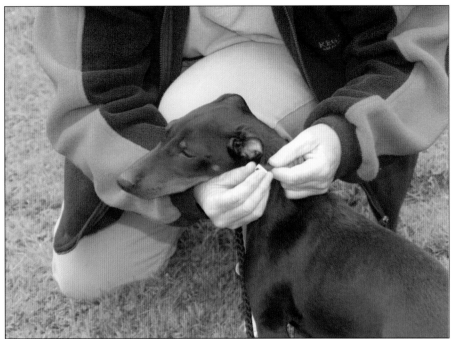

A simple buckle collar, made of nylon or cotton, is ideal for everyday use on the Manchester Terrier. Check the collar regularly to make sure it's not too tight around the dog's neck.

should be able to fit a finger between the pup and the collar. It may take some time for your pup to get used to wearing the collar, but soon he will not even notice that it is there. Choke collars are made for training, but should only be used by experienced handlers.

Food and Water Bowls

Your pup will need two bowls, one for food and one for water. You may want two sets of bowls, one for inside and one for outside, depending on where the dog will be fed and where he will be spending time. Stainless steel or sturdy plastic bowls are popular choices. Plastic bowls are more chewable. Dogs tend not to chew on the steel variety, which can be sterilised. It is important to buy sturdy bowls since anything is in danger of being chewed by puppy teeth and you do not want your dog to be constantly chewing apart his bowl (for his safety and for your purse!).

Cleaning Supplies

Until a pup is house-trained, you will be doing a lot of cleaning. Accidents will occur, which is acceptable in the beginning because the puppy does not know any better. All you can do

Your local pet shop sells an array of dishes and bowls for water and food.

is be prepared to clean up any accidents. Old rags, towels, newspapers and a safe disinfectant are good to have on hand.

BEYOND THE BASICS
The items previously discussed are the bare necessities. You will find out what else you need as you go along—grooming supplies, flea/tick protection, baby gates to partition a room, etc. These things will vary depending on your situation but it is important that you have everything you need to feed and make your Manchester Terrier comfortable in his first few days at home.

PUPPY-PROOFING YOUR HOME
Aside from making sure that your Manchester Terrier will be comfortable in your home, you also have to make sure that your home is safe for your Manchester Terrier. This means taking precautions that your pup will not get into anything he should not get into and that there is nothing within his reach that may harm him should he sniff it, chew it, inspect it, etc. This probably seems obvious since, while you are primarily concerned with your pup's safety, at the same time you do not want your belongings to be ruined. Breakables should be placed out of reach if your dog is to have full run of the house.

If he is to be limited to certain places within the house, keep any potentially dangerous items in the 'off-limits' areas. An electrical lead can pose a danger should the puppy decide to taste it—and who is going to convince a pup that it would not make a great chew toy? Leads should be fastened tightly against the wall, away from puppy teeth. If your dog is going to spend time in a crate, make sure that there is nothing near his crate that he can reach if he sticks his curious little nose or paws through the openings. Just as you would with a child, keep all household cleaners and chemicals where the pup cannot reach them.

It is also important to make sure that the outside of your home is safe. Of course your puppy should never be unsupervised, but a pup let loose in the garden will want to run and explore, and he should be granted that freedom. Do not let a fence give you a false sense of security; you would be surprised how crafty (and persistent) a dog can be in working out how to dig under and squeeze his way through small holes, or to jump or climb over a fence. The remedy is to make the fence well embedded into the ground and high enough so that it really is impossible for your dog to get over it (about 2

NATURAL TOXINS

Examine your grass and garden landscaping before bringing your puppy home. Many varieties of plants have leaves, stems or flowers that are toxic if ingested, and you can depend on a curious puppy to investigate them. Ask your vet for information on poisonous plants or research them at your library.

metres should suffice). Be sure to repair or secure any gaps in the fence. Check the fence periodically to ensure that it is in good shape and make repairs as needed; a very determined pup may return to the same spot to 'work on it' until he is able to get through.

FIRST TRIP TO THE VET

You have selected your puppy, and your home and family are ready. Now all you have to do is collect your Manchester Terrier from the breeder and the fun begins, right? Well...not so fast. Something else you need to prepare is your pup's first trip to the veterinary surgeon. Perhaps the breeder can recommend someone in the area who specialises in terriers, or maybe you know some other Manchester Terrier owners who can suggest a good vet. Either way, you should have an appointment arranged for your pup before you pick him up.

The pup's first visit will consist of an overall examination to make sure that the pup does not have any problems that are not apparent to you. The veterinary surgeon will also set up a schedule for the pup's vaccinations; the breeder will inform you of which ones the pup has already received and the vet can continue from there.

INTRODUCTION TO THE FAMILY

Everyone in the house will be excited about the puppy's coming home and will want to pet him and play with him, but it is best to make the introduction low-key so as not to overwhelm the puppy. He is apprehensive already. It is the first time he has been separated from his dam and the breeder, and the ride to your home is likely to be the first time he has been in a car. The last thing you want to do is smother him, as this will only frighten him further. This is not to say that human contact is not extremely neces-

TOXIC PLANTS

Many plants can be toxic to dogs. If you see your dog carrying a piece of vegetation in his mouth, approach him in a quiet, disinterested manner, avoid eye contact, pet him and gradually remove the plant from his mouth. Alternatively, offer him a treat and maybe he'll drop the plant on his own accord. Be sure no toxic plants are growing in your own garden or kept in your home.

sary at this stage, because this is the time when a connection between the pup and his human family is formed. Gentle petting and soothing words should help console him, as well as just putting him down and letting him explore on his own (under your watchful eye, of course).

The pup may approach the family members or may busy himself with exploring for a while. Gradually, each person should spend some time with the pup, one at a time, crouching down to get as close to the pup's level as possible and letting him sniff their hands and petting him gently. He definitely needs human attention and he needs to be touched—this is how to form an immediate bond. Just remember that the pup is

Handling the puppy and showing him signs of affection tell the puppy that he is welcomed by members of his new pack.

experiencing a lot of things for the first time, at the same time. There are new people, new noises, new smells and new things to investigate, so be gentle, be affectionate and be as comforting as you can be.

INSURANCE

Many good breeders will offer you insurance with your new puppy, which is an excellent idea. The first few weeks of insurance will probably be covered free of charge or with only minimal cost, allowing you to take up the policy when this expires. If you own a pet dog, it is sensible to take out such a policy as veterinary fees can be high, although routine vaccinations and boosters are not usually covered. Look carefully at the many options open to you before deciding which suits you best.

PUP'S FIRST NIGHT HOME

You have travelled home with your new charge safely in his crate. He's been to the vet for a thorough check-up; he's been weighed, his papers examined; perhaps he's even been vaccinated and wormed as well. He's met the family, licked the whole family, including the excited children and the less-than-happy cat. He's explored his area, his new bed, the garden and anywhere else he's been permitted. He's eaten his first meal at home and relieved

scared, cold and lonely. Be reassuring to your new family member, but this is not the time to spoil him and give in to his inevitable whining.

Puppies whine. They whine to let others know where they are and hopefully to get company out of it. Place your pup in his new bed or crate in his room and close the door. Mercifully, he may fall asleep without a peep. When the inevitable occurs, ignore the whining: he is fine. Be strong and keep his interest in mind. Do not allow yourself to feel guilty and visit the pup. He will fall asleep eventually.

Many breeders recommend placing a piece of bedding from his former home in his new bed so that he recognises the scent of his littermates. Others still advise placing a hot water bottle in his bed for warmth. This latter may be a good idea provided the pup doesn't attempt to suckle—he'll get good and wet and may not fall asleep so fast.

himself in the proper place. He's heard lots of new sounds, smelled new friends and seen more of the outside world than ever before. That was just the first day! He's worn out and is ready for bed...or so you think!

It's puppy's first night and you are ready to say 'Good night'—keep in mind that this is puppy's first night ever to be sleeping alone. His dam and littermates are no longer at paw's length and he's a bit

FEEDING TIPS
You will probably start feeding your pup the same food that he has been getting from the breeder; the breeder should give you a few days' supply to start you off. Although you should not give your pup too many treats, you will want to have puppy treats on hand for coaxing, training, rewards, etc. Be careful, though, as a small pup's calorie requirements are relatively low and a few treats can add up to almost a full day's worth of calories without the required nutrition.

HOW VACCINES WORK

If you've just bought a puppy, you surely know the importance of having your pup vaccinated, but do you understand how vaccines work? Vaccines contain the same bacteria or viruses that cause the disease you want to prevent, but they have been chemically modified so that they don't cause any harm. Instead, the vaccine causes your dog to produce antibodies that fight the harmful bacteria. Thus, if your dog is exposed to the disease in the future, the antibodies will destroy the viruses or bacteria.

Puppy's first night can be somewhat stressful for the pup and his new family. Remember that you are setting the tone of nighttime at your house. Unless you want to play with your pup every evening at 10 p.m., midnight and 2 a.m., don't initiate the habit. Your family will thank you, and eventually so will your pup!

PREVENTING PUPPY PROBLEMS

SOCIALISATION

Now that you have done all of the preparatory work and have helped your pup get accustomed to his new home and family, it is about time for you to have some fun! Socialising your Manchester Terrier pup gives you the opportunity to show off your new friend, and your pup gets to reap the benefits of being an adorable little creature that people will want to pet and, in general, think is absolutely precious!

Besides getting to know his new family, your puppy should be exposed to other people, animals and situations, but of course he must not come into close contact with dogs you don't know well until his course of injections is fully complete. Socialisation will help him become well adjusted as he grows up and less prone to being timid or fearful of the new things he will encounter. Your pup's socialisation began with the breeder but now it is your responsibility to continue it. The socialisation he receives up until the age of 12 weeks is the most critical, as this is the time when he forms his impressions of the outside world. Be especially careful during the eight-to-ten-week-old period, also known as the fear period. The interaction he receives during this time should be gentle and reassuring. Lack of socialisation can manifest itself in fear and aggression as the dog grows up. He needs lots of human contact, affection, handling and exposure to other animals.

Once your pup has received

MANNERS MATTER

During the socialisation process, a puppy should meet people, experience different environments and definitely be exposed to other canines. Through playing and interacting with other dogs, your puppy will learn lessons, ranging from controlling the pressure of his jaws by biting his littermates to the inner-workings of the canine pack that he will apply to his human relationships for the rest of his life. That is why removing a puppy from his litter too early (before eight weeks) can be detrimental to the pup's development.

his necessary vaccinations, feel free to take him out and about (on his lead, of course). Walk him around the neighbourhood, take him on your daily errands, let people pet him, let him meet other dogs and pets, etc.

Puppies do not have to try to make friends; there will be no shortage of people who will want to introduce themselves. Just make sure that you carefully supervise each meeting. If the neighbourhood children want to meet him, for example, that is great—children and pups most often make great companions. However, sometimes an excited child can unintentionally handle a pup too roughly, or an overzealous pup can playfully nip a little too hard. You want to make socialisation experiences positive ones. What a pup learns during this very formative stage will affect his attitude toward future encounters. You want your dog to be comfortable around everyone. A pup that has a bad experience with a child may grow up to be a dog that is shy around or aggressive toward children.

CONSISTENCY IN TRAINING

Dogs, being pack animals, naturally need a leader, or else they try to establish dominance in their packs. When you welcome a dog into your family, the choice of who becomes the leader and who becomes the pack is entirely up to you! Your pup's intuitive quest for dominance, coupled with the fact that puppies are irresistible, give the pup almost an unfair advantage in getting the upper hand! A pup will definitely test the waters to see what he can and cannot do. Do not give in to those pleading eyes—stand your ground when it comes to disciplining the pup and make sure that all family members do the same. It will only confuse the pup when Mother tells him to get off the sofa when he is used to sitting up there with Father to watch the nightly news. Avoid discrepancies by having all members of the household decide on the rules before the pup even comes home...and be consistent in enforcing them! Early training shapes the dog's personality, so you cannot be unclear in what you expect.

COMMON PUPPY PROBLEMS

The best way to prevent puppy problems is to be proactive in stopping an undesirable behaviour as soon as it starts. The old saying 'You can't teach an old dog new tricks' does not necessarily hold true, but it *is* true that it is much easier to discourage bad behaviour in a young developing pup than to wait until the pup's bad behaviour becomes the adult dog's bad habit. There are some problems that are especially prevalent in puppies as they develop.

NIPPING

As puppies start to teethe, they feel the need to sink their teeth into anything available... unfortunately, that includes your fingers, arms, hair and toes. You may find this behaviour cute for the first five seconds...until you feel just how sharp those puppy teeth are. This is something you want to discourage immediately and consistently with a firm 'No!'

SOCIALISATION PERIOD

The socialisation period for puppies is from age 8 to 16 weeks. This is the time when puppies need to leave their birth family and take up residence with their new owners, where they will meet many new people, other pets, etc. Failure to be adequately socialised can cause the dog to grow up fearing others and being shy and unfriendly due to a lack of self-confidence.

(or whatever number of firm 'Nos' it takes for him to understand that you mean business). Then replace your finger with an appropriate chew toy. While this behaviour is merely annoying when the dog is young, it can become dangerous as your Manchester Terrier's adult teeth grow in and his jaws develop, and he continues to think it is okay to gnaw on human appendages. Your Manchester Terrier does not mean any harm with a friendly nip, but he also does not know his own strength.

CRYING/WHINING

Your pup will often cry, whine, whimper, howl or make some type of commotion when he is left alone. This is basically his way of calling out for attention to make sure that you know he is there and that you have not forgotten about him. He feels insecure when he is left alone, when you are out of the house and he is in his crate or when you are in another part of the house and he cannot see you. The noise he is making is an expression of the anxiety he feels at being alone, so he needs to be taught that being alone is okay. You are not actually training the dog to stop making noise, you are training him to feel comfortable when he is alone and thus removing the need for him to make the noise. This is where the crate with cosy bedding and a toy comes in handy. You want to know that he is safe when you are not there to supervise, and you know that he will be safe in his crate rather than roaming freely about the house. In order for the pup to stay in his crate without making a fuss, he needs to be comfortable in his crate. On that note, it is extremely important that the crate is never used as a form of punishment, or the pup will develop a negative association with the crate.

Accustom the pup to the crate in short, gradually increasing time intervals in which you put him in the crate, maybe with a treat, and stay in the room with him. If he cries or makes a fuss, do not go to him, but stay in his sight. Gradually he will realise that staying in his crate is okay without your help, and it will not be so traumatic for him when you are not around. You may want to leave the radio on softly when you leave the house; the sound of human voices may be comforting to him.

CHEWING TIPS

Chewing goes hand in hand with nipping in the sense that a teething puppy is always looking for a way to soothe his aching gums. In this case, instead of chewing on you, he may have taken a liking to your favourite shoe or something else that he should not be chewing. Again, realise that this is a normal canine behaviour that does not need to be discouraged, only redirected. Your pup just needs to be taught what is acceptable to chew on and what is off limits. Consistently tell him 'No' when you catch him chewing on something forbidden and give him a chew toy.

Conversely, praise him when you catch him chewing on something appropriate. In this way you are discouraging the inappropriate behaviour and reinforcing the desired behaviour. The puppy chewing should stop after his adult teeth have come in, but an adult dog continues to chew for various reasons—perhaps because he is bored, needs to relieve tension or just likes to chew. That is why it is important to redirect his chewing when he is still young.

DIETARY AND FEEDING CONSIDERATIONS

Today the choices of food for your Manchester Terrier are many and varied. There are simply dozens of brands of food in all sorts of flavours and textures, ranging from puppy diets to those for veterans. There are even hypoallergenic and low-calorie diets available. Because your Manchester Terrier's food has a bearing on coat, health and temperament, it is essential that the most suitable diet is selected for a Manchester Terrier of his age. It is fair to say, however, that even experienced owners can be perplexed by the enormous range of foods available. Only under-standing what is best for your dog will help you reach a valued decision.

Dog foods are produced in three basic types: dried, semi-moist and tinned. Dried foods are useful for the cost-conscious for overall they tend to be less expensive than semi-moist or tinned. They also contain the least fat and the most preserva-tives. In general, tinned foods are made up of 60–70% water, while semi-moist ones often contain so much sugar that they are perhaps the least preferred by owners, even though their dogs seem to like them.

When selecting your dog's diet, three stages of development must be considered: the puppy

FOOD STORAGE

You must store your dried dog food carefully. Open packages of dog food quickly lose their vitamin value, usually within 90 days of being opened. Mould spores and vermin could also contaminate the food.

stage, the adult stage and the veteran stage.

PUPPY STAGE

Puppies instinctively want to suck milk from their mother's teats, and a normal puppy will exhibit this behaviour from just a few moments following birth. If puppies do not attempt to suckle within the first half-hour or so, they should be encouraged to do so by placing them on the nipples, having selected ones with plenty of milk. This early milk supply is important in providing colostrum to protect the puppies during the first eight to ten weeks of their lives. Although a mother's milk is much better than any milk formula, despite there being some excellent ones available, if the puppies do not feed, the breeder will have to hand-feed them himself. For those with less experience, advice from a veterinary surgeon is important so that not only the right quantity of milk is fed but also that of correct quality, fed at suitably frequent intervals, usually every two hours during the first few days of life.

Puppies should be allowed to nurse from their dam for about the first six weeks, although from the third or fourth week the breeder should begin to introduce small portions of suitable solid food. Most breeders like to

FOOD PREFERENCE

Selecting the best dog food is difficult. There is no majority consensus among veterinary scientists as to the value of nutrient analyses (protein, fat, fibre, moisture, ash, cholesterol, minerals, etc.). All agree that feeding trials are what matter most, but you also have to consider the individual dog. The dog's weight, age and activity level, and what pleases his taste, all must be considered. It is probably best to take the advice of your veterinary surgeon. Every dog's dietary requirements vary, even during the lifetime of a particular dog.

If your dog is fed a good dried food, it does not require supplements of meat or vegetables. Dogs do appreciate a little variety in their diets, so you may choose to stay with the same brand but vary the flavour. Alternatively, you may wish to add a little flavoured stock to give a difference to the taste.

introduce alternate milk and meat meals initially, building up to weaning time.

By the time the puppies are seven or a maximum of eight weeks old, they should be fully weaned and fed solely on a proprietary puppy food. Selection of the most suitable, good-quality diet at this time is essential, for a puppy's fastest growth rate is during the first year of life. Breeders and veterinary surgeons are usually able to offer advice in this regard and, although the frequency of meals will have been reduced over time, only when a young dog has reached the age of about 12 months should an adult diet be fed.

Puppy and junior diets should be well balanced for the needs of your dog so that, except in certain circumstances, additional vitamins, minerals and proteins will not be required.

ADULT DIETS

A dog is considered an adult when he has stopped growing, so in general the diet of a Manchester Terrier can be changed to an adult one at about 12 months of age. Again you should rely upon your veterinary surgeon or breeder to recommend an acceptable maintenance diet. Major dog-food manufacturers specialise in this type of food, and it is merely necessary for you to select the one best suited to your dog's needs. Active dogs have different requirements from sedate dogs.

VETERAN DIETS

As dogs get older, their metabolism changes. The older dog usually exercises less, moves more slowly and sleeps more. This change in lifestyle and physiological performance requires a change in diet. Since these changes take place slowly, they might not be recognisable. What is easily recognisable is

---

TEST FOR PROPER DIET

A good test for proper diet is the colour, odour and firmness of your dog's stool. An healthy dog usually produces three semi-hard stools per day. The stools should have no unpleasant odour. They should be the same colour from excretion to excretion.

weight gain. By continuing to feed your dog an adult-maintenance diet when he is slowing down metabolically, your dog will gain weight. Obesity in an older dog compounds the health problems that already accompany old age.

As your dog gets older, few of his organs function up to par. The kidneys slow down and the intestines become less efficient. These age-related factors are best handled with a change in diet and a change in feeding schedule to give smaller portions that are more easily digested.

There is no single best diet for every older dog. While many dogs do well on light or veteran diets, other dogs do better on puppy diets or special premium diets such as lamb and rice. Be sensitive to your veteran Manchester Terrier's diet and this will help control other problems that may arise with your old friend.

WATER

Just as your dog needs proper nutrition from his food, water is an essential 'nutrient' as well. Water keeps the dog's body properly hydrated and promotes normal function of the body's systems. During house-training it is necessary to keep an eye on how much water your Manchester Terrier is drinking, but, once he is reliably trained,

CHANGE IN DIET

As your dog's caretaker, you know the importance of keeping his diet consistent, but sometimes when you run out of food or if you're on holiday, you have to make a change quickly. Some dogs will experience digestive problems, but most will not. If you are planning on changing your dog's menu, do so gradually to ensure that your dog will not have any problems. Over a period of four to five days, slowly add some new food to your dog's old food, increasing the percentage of new food each day.

he should have access to clean fresh water at all times, especially if you feed dried food. Make certain that the dog's water bowl is clean, and change the water often.

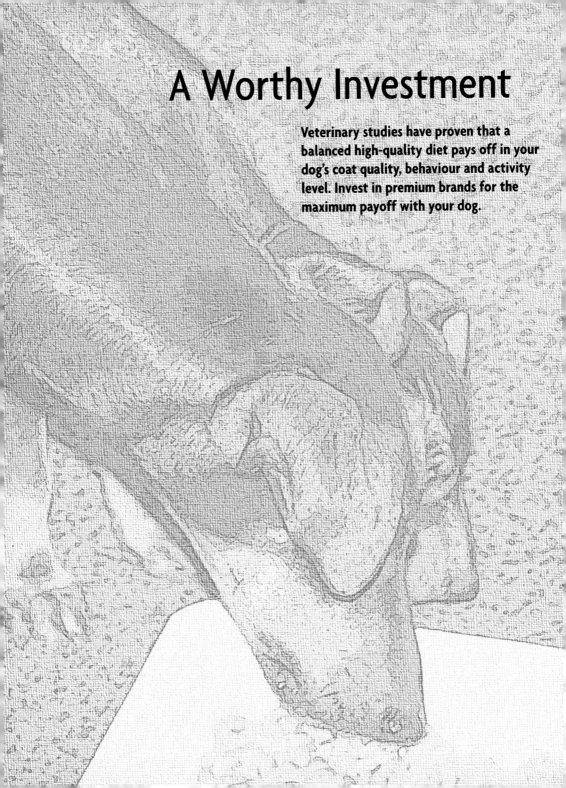

A Worthy Investment

Veterinary studies have proven that a balanced high-quality diet pays off in your dog's coat quality, behaviour and activity level. Invest in premium brands for the maximum payoff with your dog.

EXERCISE

The Manchester Terrier, of course, was bred to be a working hunting dog, and as such requires a reasonable amount of daily physical activity, though not as much as many people expect. Not too many Manchesters today are chasing a gang of rats into the river, but these same handsome pets do need to get outside and run and play. Manchesters will be happy to be included in any activity the owner enjoys, whether that's gardening, walking or reading a book. Just as these dogs are active of body, they are also active of mind and therefore creative! You do not want an overly creative Manchester finding ways of amusing himself and exercising in your home. You will be glad you got him outdoors to stretch his legs!

Regular walks, play sessions in the garden and letting the dog run free in an enclosed area under your supervision are sufficient forms of exercise for the Manchester Terrier. For those who are more ambitious, you will find that your Manchester Terrier also enjoys an occasional hike, running by your bicycle, games of fetch or even a swim! Of course, all of these activities are best when the owner is actively participating.

Bear in mind that an overweight dog should never be suddenly over-exercised; instead

DRINK, DRANK, DRUNK—MAKE IT A DOUBLE

In both humans and dogs, as well as other living organisms, water forms the major part of nearly every body tissue. Naturally, we take water for granted, but without it, life as we know it would cease.

For dogs, water is needed to keep their bodies functioning biochemically. Additionally, water is needed to replace the water lost while panting. Unlike humans, who are able to sweat to dissipate heat, dogs must pant to cool down, thereby losing the vital water that their bodies need to regulate their body temperatures. Humans lose electrolyte-containing products and other body-fluid components through sweating; dogs do not lose anything except water.

Water is essential always, but especially so when the weather is hot or humid or when your dog is exercising or working vigorously.

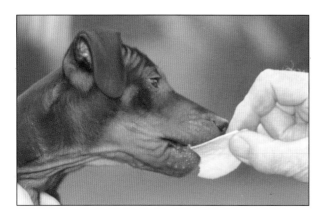

Although it may be tempting to share your snack with your dog, don't do it! Feeding 'people food' can lead to obesity and other health problems in dogs, as well as to behaviour issues like begging.

THE CANINE GOURMET

Your dog does not prefer a fresh bone. Indeed, he wants it properly aged and, if given such a treat indoors, he is more likely to try to bury it in the carpet than he is to settle in for a good chew! If you have a garden, give him such delicacies outside and guide him to a place suitable for his 'bone yard.' He will carefully place the treasure in its earthy vault and seemingly forget about it. Trust me, his seeming distaste or lack of thanks for your thoughtfulness is not that at all. He will return in a few days to inspect the bone, perhaps to re-bury it, and when it is just right, he will relish it as much as you do that cooked-to-perfection steak. If he is in a concrete or bricked kennel run, he will be especially frustrated at the hopelessness of the situation. He will vacillate between ignoring it completely, giving it a few licks to speed the curing process with saliva, and trying to hide it behind the water bowl! When the bone has aged a bit, he will set to work on it.

he should be encouraged to increase exercise slowly. Not only is exercise essential to keep the dog's body fit, it is essential to his mental well-being. A bored dog will find something to do, which often manifests itself in some type of destructive behaviour. In this sense, exercise is essential for the owner's mental well-being as well!

GROOMING

Do understand when purchasing a dog that you have the responsibility of maintaining your dog. Think of it in terms of your child—you bath your youngster, comb his hair and put a clean set of clothes on him. The end product is that you have a child that smells good and looks nice, and that you enjoy having in your company. It is the same with your dog—keep the dog brushed, cleaned and trimmed, and you will find it a pleasure to be in his company.

Here are the tools that you will need to groom properly:
1. A sturdy table, with a non-slippery surface. The height of the table is critical for the comfort of your back. You should consider a grooming arm (a "hanger" with a "noose"). Your dog will now be comfortable even if confined and you will be able to work on the dog.
2. A bristle brush or hound glove, a good, sharp pair of scissors and a toenail trimmer.

To start: Set your dog on the table and put the lead around his neck. Have your lead up behind the dog's ears and have it taut when you fasten it to your eye hook. Do not walk away and leave your dog unattended, as he can jump off the table and be left dangling from the lead with his feet scrambling around in the air. Grooming for a Manchester Terrier consists of primarily a weekly once-over. Brush him down with the bristle brush or hound glove, then take a damp wash cloth and wipe down the entire body.

Once or twice a year, you may want to put in the laundry tub and give him a bath. Most breeders advise against frequent bathing as it dries out the coat's natural oils. Unless your dog has been rolling in muck, keep bathing to a minimum. You will find that an occasional bath will loosen any dead coat, so after the bath be sure to brush him out

Give your Manchester Terrier ample time to exercise every day. The breed does not require as much exercise as you might imagine, thus making it ideal for moderately active people.

Manchesters have excellent noses, which often lead them to mischief, including eating discarded food and playing in muck.

some other hairdressing to give his coat a high gloss. Trimming for show will be minimal and the purpose will be to neaten up the dog. Smooth-coated dogs are low-maintenance and those of us who own one appreciate it!

Ear Cleaning

The ears should be kept clean with a cotton wipe and ear powder made especially for dogs. Be on the lookout for any signs of infection or ear-mite infestation. If your Manchester Terrier has been shaking his head or scratching at his ears frequently, this usually indicates a problem. If his ears have an unusual odour, this is a sure sign of mite infestation or infection, and a signal to have his ears checked by your veterinary surgeon.

thoroughly as this will clean out any dead undercoat. After the dog is bathed, it is also a good time to trim the toenails as they will be soft and easier to trim. You may want to trim the whiskers to the skin as this will give the dog a neat, clean-cut look. Wipe him dry with a towel or use a blaster, and if it is a nice, sunny day, you may want to put him outside in a clean area to dry naturally.

Your pet should be brushed weekly and bathed as needed, and his nails should be trimmed every month or so. Follow this easy plan and your dog will be clean, smelling good and pleasant to have around.

If you are showing your Manchester, you may want to rub the dog down with a pomade or

---

WISDOM FROM YESTERYEAR
Holland Buckley wrote in 1913: 'Most people wash their dogs regularly. Unless preparing a puppy for a special purpose, do not bath him at all, at least not artificially, but get him used to swimming in a pond or the river, never forgetting to give him a good gallop and a rub down afterwards. A few minutes spent each day with a comb and a dandy brush will keep the coat in tip-top condition, and the skin supple and healthy.'

NAIL CLIPPING

Your Manchester Terrier should be accustomed to having his nails trimmed at an early age, since it will be a part of your maintenance routine throughout his life. Not only does it look nicer, but long nails can scratch someone unintentionally. Also, a long nail has a better chance of ripping and bleeding, or causing the feet to spread. A good rule of thumb is that if you can hear your dog's nails clicking on the floor when he walks, his nails are too long.

Before you start cutting, make sure you can identify the 'quick' in each nail. The quick is a blood vessel that runs through the centre of each nail and grows rather close to the end. It will bleed if accidentally cut, which will be quite painful for the dog as it contains nerve endings.

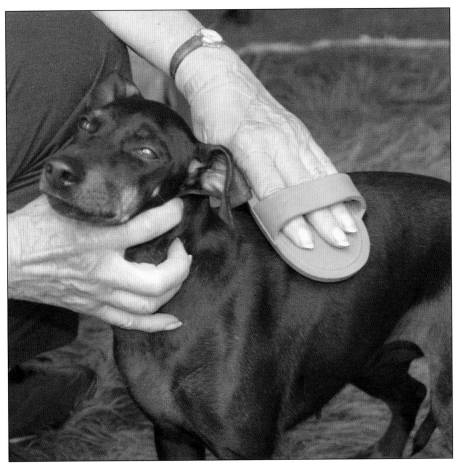

A rubber curry brush or hound glove can be used to keep the Manchester's sleek coat shiny and clean.

Finish off the coat with a chamois to give it a little extra sheen.

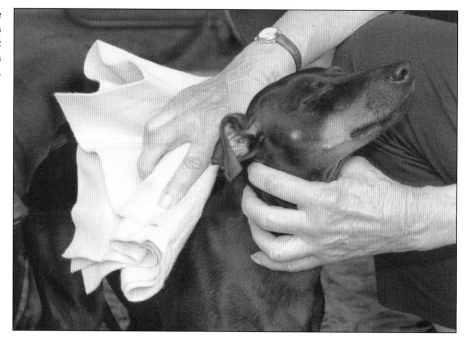

The ears should be cleaned with a soft cotton wipe and ear cleanser (available from your pet shop). Advise your veterinary surgeon of any odours or mites that you might find.

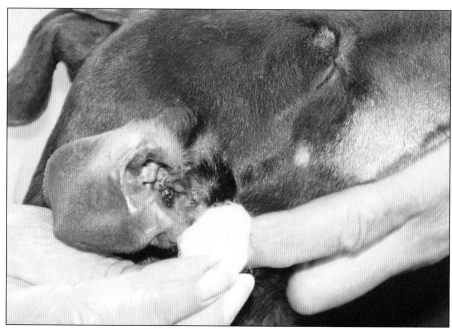

Keep some type of clotting agent on hand, such as a styptic pencil or styptic powder (the type used for shaving). This will stop the bleeding quickly when applied to the end of the cut nail. Do not panic if you cut the quick, just stop the bleeding and talk soothingly to your dog. Once he has calmed down, move on to the next nail. It is better to clip the tips, particularly with black-nailed dogs, and then use a fairly rough file to finish off the nail.

Hold your pup steady as you begin trimming his nails; you do not want him to make any sudden movements or run away. Talk to him soothingly and stroke him as you clip. Holding his foot in your hand, simply take off the end of each nail in one quick clip. You can purchase nail clippers that are specially made for dogs; you can probably find them wherever you buy pet supplies.

TRAVELLING WITH YOUR DOG

CAR TRAVEL

You should accustom your Manchester Terrier to riding in a car at an early age. You may or may not take him in the car often, but at the very least he will need to go to the vet and you do not want these trips to be traumatic for the dog or troublesome for you. The safest way for a dog to ride in the car is in his crate. If he uses a crate in the house, you

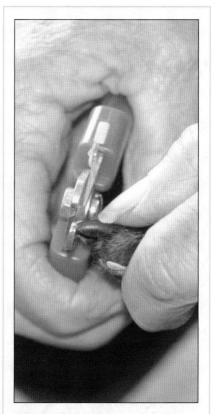

PEDICURE TIP
A dog that spends a lot of time outside on a hard surface, such as cement or pavement, will have his nails naturally worn down and may not need to have them trimmed as often, except maybe in the colder months when he is not outside as much. Regardless, it is best to get your dog accustomed to the nail-trimming procedure at an early age so that he is used to it. Some dogs are especially sensitive about having their feet touched, but if a dog has experienced it since puppyhood, it should not bother him.

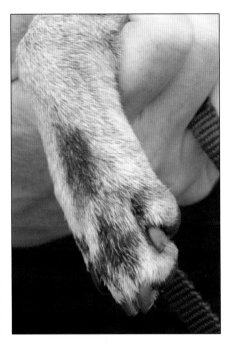

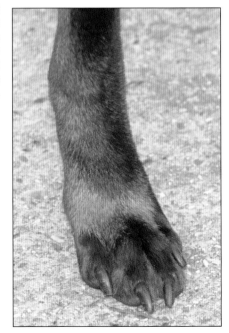

Keep your Manchester's nails cut short. They should not be clicking on the floor as the dog walks. When accustomed as a puppy, your Manchester will learn to tolerate his pedicure.

Nail Maintenance

Nail Casing

Quick

Cut Line

Dark-Coloured Nails

With black or dark nails, it's best to clip only the tip of the nail or to use a file.

Light-Coloured Nails

In light-coloured nails, clipping is much simpler because you can see the vein (or quick) that grows inside the casing.

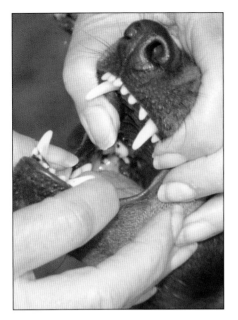

The Manchester's teeth should be white and large for the size of the mouth, a characteristic of all terrier breeds.

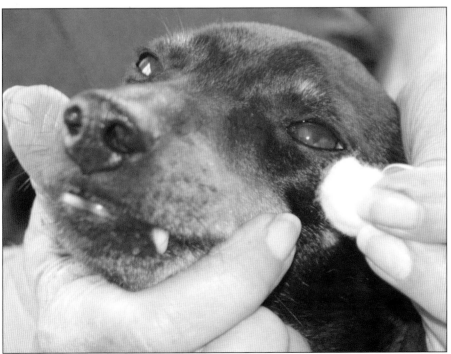

Tear stains can be removed with tear-stain remover and a soft, damp cotton wipe.

If you prefer not to have your Manchester Terrier travel in his crate, consider using partitions to keep the dog in the rear part of your vehicle.

can use the same crate for travel.

Put the pup in the crate and see how he reacts. If he seems uneasy, you can have a passenger hold him on his lap while you drive. Another option is a specially made safety harness for dogs, which straps the dog in much like a seat belt. Do not let the dog roam loose in the vehicle—this is very dangerous! If you should stop short, your dog can be thrown and injured. If the dog starts climbing on you and pestering you while you are driving, you will not be able to concentrate on the road. It is an unsafe situation for everyone—human and canine.

For long trips, be prepared to stop to let the dog relieve himself. Take with you whatever you need to clean up after him, including some paper kitchen towels and perhaps some old towelling for use should he have a toileting accident in the car or suffer from travel sickness.

TRAVEL TIP

Never leave your dog alone in the car. In hot weather, your dog can die from the high temperature inside a closed vehicle; even a car parked in the shade can heat up very quickly. Leaving the window open is dangerous as well since the dog can hurt himself trying to get out.

AIR TRAVEL

While it is possible to take a dog on a flight within Britain, this is fairly unusual and advance permission is always required. The dog will be required to travel in a fibreglass crate and you should always check in advance with the airline regarding specific requirements. To help the dog be at ease, put one of his favourite toys in the crate with him. Do not feed the dog for several hours before the trip to minimise his need to relieve himself. However, certain regulations specify that water must always be made available to the dog in the crate.

Make sure your dog is properly identified and that your contact information appears on his ID tags and on his crate. Animals travel in a different area of the plane from human passenger, so every rule must be strictly followed so as to prevent the risk of getting separated from your dog.

BOARDING AND HOLIDAYS

So you want to take a family holiday—and you want to include *all* members of the family. You would probably make arrangements for accommodation ahead of time anyway, but this is especially important when travelling with a dog. You do not want to make an overnight stop at the only place around for miles and find out that they do not allow dogs. Also, you do not want to reserve a place for your family without confirming that you are travelling with a dog because, if it is against their policy, you may not have a place to stay.

Alternatively, if you are travelling and choose not to bring your Manchester Terrier, you will have to make arrangements for him while you are away. Some options are to take him to a friend's house to stay while you

TRAVEL ALERT

When you travel with your dog, it's a good idea to take along water from home or to buy bottled water for the trip. In areas where water is sometimes chemically treated and sometimes comes right out of the ground, you can prevent adverse reactions to this essential part of your dog's diet.

are gone, to have a trusted neighbour pop in often or stay at your house or to bring your dog to a reputable boarding kennel. If you choose to board him at a kennel, you should visit in advance to see the facilities provided, how clean they are and where the dogs are kept. Talk to some of the employees and see how they treat the dogs—do they spend time with the dogs, play with them, exercise them, etc.? Also find out the kennel's policy on vaccinations and what they require. This is for all of the dogs' safety, since when dogs are kept together, there is a greater risk of diseases being passed from dog to dog.

IDENTIFICATION

Your Manchester Terrier is your valued companion and friend.

MOTION SICKNESS

*If life is a motorway...*your dog may not want to come along for the ride! Some dogs experience motion sickness in cars that leads to excessive salivation and even vomiting. In most cases, your dog will fare better in the familiar, safe confines of his crate. To desensitise your dog, try going on several short jaunts before trying a long trip. If your dog experiences distress when riding in the vehicle, drive with him only when absolutely necessary, and do not feed him or give him water before you go.

That is why you always keep a close eye on him and you have made sure that he cannot escape from the garden or wriggle out of his collar and run away from you. However, accidents can happen and there may come a time when your dog unexpectedly gets separated from you. If this unfortunate event should occur, the first thing on your mind will be finding him. Proper identification, including an ID tag, and possibly a tattoo and a microchip, will increase the chances of his being returned to you safely and quickly.

IDENTIFICATION OPTIONS

As puppies become more and more expensive, especially those puppies of high quality for showing and/or breeding, they have a greater chance of being stolen. The usual collar dog tag is, of course, easily removed. But there are two permanent techniques that have become widely used for identification.

The puppy microchip implantation involves the injection of a small microchip, about the size of a corn kernel, under the skin of the dog. If your dog shows up at a clinic or shelter, or is offered for resale under less than savoury circumstances, he can be positively identified by the microchip. The microchip is scanned, and a registry quickly identifies you as the owner. This is not only protection against theft, but should the dog run away or go chasing a squirrel and become lost, you have a fair chance of his being returned to you.

Tattooing is always done on the dog's ear. The number tattooed can be your telephone number, your dog's registration number or any other number that you can easily memorise. When professional dog thieves see a tattooed dog, they usually lose interest. For the safety of our dogs, no laboratory facility or dog broker will accept a tattooed dog as stock. Both microchipping and tattooing can be done at your local veterinary clinic.

No dog should ever be without his identification tag securely attached to his everyday collar.

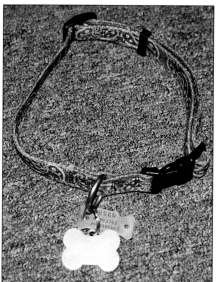

TRAINING YOUR
MANCHESTER TERRIER

Living with an untrained dog is a lot like owning a piano that you do not know how to play—it is a nice object to look at, but it does not do much more than that to bring you pleasure. Now try taking piano lessons and suddenly the piano comes alive and brings forth magical sounds and rhythms that set your heart singing and your body swaying.

The same is true with your Manchester. Any dog is a big responsibility and, if not trained sensibly, may develop unacceptable behaviour that annoys you or could even cause family friction. Manchester breeders are the first to point out that their breed requires strict training, as the breed, like its many other earthdog relatives, can be a bit stubborn. Terriers are not the first choice of obedience trainers, as they can be 'too smart' for the rest of the class (or simply significantly less interested).

To train your Manchester, you would be well advised to enrol in an obedience class with an instructor who has experience (and patience) with terriers. Teach your Manchester good

REAP THE REWARDS
If you start with a normal, healthy dog and give him time, patience and some carefully executed lessons, you will reap the rewards of that training for the life of the dog. And what a life it will be! The two of you will find immeasurable pleasure in the companionship you have built together with love, respect and understanding.

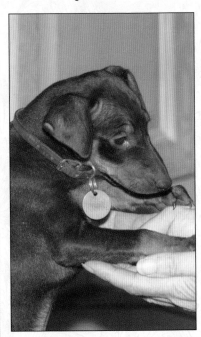

manners as you learn how and why he behaves the way he does. Find out how to communicate with your dog and how to recognise and understand his communications with you. Suddenly the dog takes on a new role in your life—he is clever, interesting, well-behaved and fun to be with. He demonstrates his bond of devotion to you daily. In other words, your Manchester does wonders for your ego because he constantly reminds you that you are not only his leader, you are his hero!

Those involved with teaching dog obedience and counselling owners about their dogs' behaviour have discovered some interesting facts about dog ownership. For example, training dogs when they are puppies results in the highest rate of success in developing well-mannered and well-adjusted adult dogs. Training an older dog, from six months to six years of age, can produce almost equal results, providing that the owner accepts the dog's slower rate of learning capability and is willing to work patiently to help the dog succeed at developing to his fullest potential. Unfortunately, many owners of untrained adult dogs lack the patience factor, so they do not persist until their dogs are successful at learning particular behaviours.

Training a puppy aged 10 to 16 weeks (20 weeks at the most)

PARENTAL GUIDANCE
Training a dog is a life experience. Many parents admit that much of what they know about raising children they learned from caring for their dogs. Dogs respond to love, fairness and guidance, just as children do. Become a good dog owner and you may become an even better parent.

is like working with a dry sponge in a pool of water. The pup soaks up whatever you show him and constantly looks for more things to do and learn. At this early age, his body is not yet producing hormones, and therein lies the reason for such a high rate of success. Without hormones, he is focused on his owners and not particularly interested in investigating other places, dogs, people, etc. You are his leader: his

FAMILY TIES

If you have other pets in the home and/or interact often with the pets of friends and other family members, your pup will respond to those pets in much the same manner as you do. It is only when you show fear of or resentment toward another animal that he will act fearful or unfriendly.

provider of food, water, shelter and security. He latches onto you and wants to stay close. He will usually follow you from room to room, will not let you out of his sight when you are outdoors with him and will respond in like manner to the people and animals you encounter. If you greet a friend warmly, he will be happy to greet the person as well. If, however, you are hesitant or anxious about the approach of a stranger, he will respond accordingly to you.

Once the puppy begins to produce hormones, his natural curiosity emerges and he begins to investigate the world around him. It is at this time when you may notice that the untrained dog begins to wander away from you and even ignore your commands to stay close. When this behaviour becomes a problem, the owner has two choices: get rid of the dog or train him. It is strongly urged that you choose the latter option.

There usually will be classes within a reasonable distance from your home, but you can also do a lot to train your dog yourself. Sometimes there are classes available but the tuition is too costly. Whatever the circumstances, the solution to training your Manchester without formal obedience classes lies within the pages of this book. This chapter is devoted to helping you train your Manchester at home. If the recommended procedures are followed faithfully, you may expect positive results that will prove rewarding both to you and your dog.

Whether your new charge is a puppy or a mature adult, the methods of teaching and the techniques we use in training basic behaviours are the same. After all, no dog, whether puppy or adult, likes harsh or inhumane

THINK BEFORE YOU BARK

Dogs are sensitive to their masters' moods and emotions. Use your voice wisely when communicating with your dog. Never raise your voice at your dog unless you are trying to correct him. 'Barking' at your dog can become as meaningless as 'dogspeak' is to you.

methods. All creatures, however, respond favourably to gentle motivational methods and sincere praise and encouragement. Now let us get started.

HOUSE-TRAINING

You can train a puppy to relieve himself wherever you choose, but this must be somewhere suitable. You should bear in mind from the outset that when your puppy is old enough to go out in public places, any canine droppings must be removed at once. You will always have to carry with you a small plastic bag or 'poop-scoop.' Outdoor training includes such surfaces as grass, soil and cement. Indoor training usually means training your dog to newspaper. When deciding on the surface and location that you will

Treat your adult or puppy fairly and he will respond appropriately. Manchester Terriers are especially sensitive to the tone of their master's voice.

want your Manchester to use, be sure it is going to be permanent. Training your dog to grass and then changing your mind two months later is extremely difficult for both dog and owner.

Next, choose the command you will use each and every time you want your puppy to void. 'Hurry up' and 'Toilet' are examples of commands commonly used by dog owners.

Get in the habit of giving the puppy your chosen relief command before you take him out. That way, when he becomes an adult, you will be able to determine if he wants to go out when you ask him. A confirmation will be signs of interest, such as wagging his tail, watching you intently, going to the door, etc.

PUPPY'S NEEDS
Your puppy needs to relieve himself after play periods, after each meal, after he has been sleeping and at any time he indicates that he is looking for a place to urinate or defecate. The urinary and intestinal tract muscles of very young puppies are not fully developed.

Grass is every dog's favourite relief site—naturally! This Manchester puppy is enjoying the scent of the grass or perhaps that of a passing rodent.

CANINE DEVELOPMENT TIMETABLE

It is important to understand how and at what age a puppy develops into adulthood.
If you are a puppy owner, consult the following Canine Development Timetable to
determine the stage of development your puppy is currently experiencing.
This knowledge will help you as you work with the puppy in the weeks and months ahead.

Period	Age	Characteristics
FIRST TO THIRD	BIRTH TO SEVEN WEEKS	Puppy needs food, sleep and warmth, and responds to simple and gentle touching. Needs mother for security and disciplining. Needs littermates for learning and interacting with other dogs. Pup learns to function within a pack and learns pack order of dominance. Begin socialising with adults and children for short periods. Begins to become aware of his environment.
FOURTH	EIGHT TO TWELVE WEEKS	Brain is fully developed. Needs socialising with outside world. Remove from mother and littermates. Needs to change from canine pack to human pack. Human dominance necessary. Fear period occurs between 8 and 12 weeks. Avoid fright and pain.
FIFTH	THIRTEEN TO SIXTEEN WEEKS	Training and formal obedience should begin. Less association with other dogs, more with people, places, situations. Period will pass easily if you remember this is pup's change-to-adolescence time. Be firm and fair. Flight instinct prominent. Permissiveness and over-disciplining can do permanent damage. Praise for good behaviour.
JUVENILE	FOUR TO EIGHT MONTHS	Another fear period about 7 to 8 months of age. It passes quickly, but be cautious of fright and pain. Sexual maturity reached. Dominant traits established. Dog should understand sit, down, come and stay by now.

NOTE: THESE ARE APPROXIMATE TIME FRAMES. ALLOW FOR INDIVIDUAL DIFFERENCES IN PUPPIES.

Allowing your Manchester puppy free run of the house from the onset is not a good idea. Your puppy will inspect and taste everything he encounters.

SAFETY FIRST

While it may seem that the most important things to your dog are eating, sleeping and chewing the upholstery on your furniture, his first concern is actually safety. The domesticated dogs we keep as companions have the same pack instinct as their ancestors who ran free thousands of years ago. Because of this pack instinct, your dog wants to know that he and his pack are not in danger of being harmed, and that his pack has a strong, capable leader. You must establish yourself as the leader early on in your relationship. That way your dog will trust that you will take care of him and the pack, and he will accept your commands without question.

Therefore, like human babies, puppies need to relieve themselves frequently.

Take your puppy out often—every hour for an eight-week-old, for example, and always immediately after sleeping and eating. The older the puppy, the less often he will need to relieve himself. Finally, as a mature healthy adult, he will require only three to five relief trips per day.

HOUSING

Since the types of housing and control you provide for your puppy have a direct relationship on the success of house-training, we consider the various aspects of both before we begin training.

HONOUR AND OBEY

Dogs are the most honourable animals in existence. They consider another species (humans) as their own. They interface with you. You are their leader. Puppies perceive children to be on their level; their actions around small children are different from their behaviour around their adult masters.

Taking a new puppy home and turning him loose in your house can be compared to turning a child loose in an exhibition centre and telling the child that the place is all his! The sheer enormity of the place would be too much for him to handle.

Instead, offer the puppy clearly defined areas where he can play, sleep, eat and live. A room of the house where the family gathers is the most obvious choice. Puppies are social animals and need to feel a part of the pack right from the start. Hearing your voice, watching you while you are doing things and smelling you nearby are all positive reinforcers that he is now a member of your pack. Usually a family room, the kitchen or a nearby adjoining breakfast area is ideal for providing safety and security for both puppy and owner.

Within that room, there should be a smaller area that the puppy can call his own. An alcove, a wire or fibreglass dog crate or a gated (not boarded!) corner from which he can view the activities of his new family

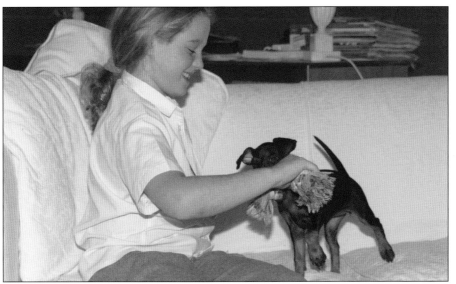

Rope toys are popular devices for dogs, but do not initiate games of tug-o-war with a young puppy. Challenge games are not recommended as they incite the dog's desire to overcome his master.

Your Manchester Terrier adult will be very comfortable in his crate, providing that it is large enough and the dog has been accustomed to it since puppyhood.

These two littermates are enjoying a game of 'who's the top dog' in a crate. Select a crate large enough that it will accommodate your Manchester once he is fully grown.

will be fine. The size of the area or crate is the key factor here. The area must be large enough for the puppy to lie down and stretch out as well as stand up without rubbing his head on the top, yet small enough so that he cannot relieve himself at one end and sleep at the other without coming into contact with his droppings during the house-training process. The designated area should contain clean bedding and a toy. Water must always be available, in a non-spill container.

Dogs are, by nature, clean animals and will not remain close to their relief areas unless forced to do so. In those cases, they then become dirty dogs and usually remain that way for life.

CONTROL

By *control*, we mean helping the puppy to create a lifestyle pattern that will be compatible to that of his human pack (you!). Just as we guide little children to learn our way of life, we must show the puppy when it is time to play, eat, sleep, exercise and even entertain himself.

Your puppy should always sleep in his crate. He should also learn that, during times of house-hold confusion and excessive human activity such as at break-fast when family members are preparing for the day, he can play by himself in relative safety and

PRACTICE MAKES PERFECT!

• Have training lessons with your dog every day in several short segments—three to five times a day for a few minutes at a time is ideal.

• Do not have long practice sessions. The dog will become easily bored.

• Never practise when you are tired, ill, worried or in an otherwise negative mood. This will transmit to the dog and may have an adverse effect on his performance.

Think fun, short and above all *positive!* End each session on an high note, rather than a failed exercise, and make sure to give a lot of praise. Enjoy the training and help your dog enjoy it, too.

comfort in his designated area. Each time you leave the puppy alone, he should understand exactly where he is to stay. Puppies are chewers. They cannot tell the difference between things like lamp and television leads, shoes, table legs, etc. Chewing into a television lead, for example, can be fatal to the puppy, while a shorted wire can start a fire in the house.

If the puppy chews on the arm of the chair when he is alone, you will probably discipline him angrily when you get

THE SUCCESS METHOD

Success that comes by luck is usually short-lived. Success that comes by well-thought-out proven methods is often more easily achieved and permanent. This is the Success Method. It is designed to give you, the puppy owner, a simple yet proven way to help your puppy develop clean living habits and a feeling of security in his new environment.

6 Steps to Successful Crate Training

1 Tell the puppy 'Crate time!' and place him in the crate with a small treat (a piece of cheese or half of a biscuit). Let him stay in the crate for five minutes while you are in the same room. Then release him and praise lavishly. Never release him when he is fussing. Wait until he is quiet before you let him out.

2 Repeat Step 1 several times a day.

3 The next day, place the puppy in the crate as before. Let him stay there for ten minutes. Do this several times.

4 Continue building time in five-minute increments until the puppy stays in his crate for 30 minutes with you in the room. Always take him to his relief area after prolonged periods in his crate.

5 Now go back to Step 1 and let the puppy stay in his crate for five minutes, this time while you are out of the room.

6 Once again, build crate time in five-minute increments with you out of the room. When the puppy will stay willingly in his crate (he may even fall asleep!) for 30 minutes with you out of the room, he will be ready to stay in it for several hours at a time.

home. Thus, he makes the association that your coming home means he is going to be punished. (He will not remember chewing the chair and is incapable of making the association of the discipline with his naughty deed.) Crating the pup prevents dangerous and/or destructive behaviour.

Times of excitement, such as friends' visits, family parties, etc., can be fun for the puppy, providing he can view the activities from the security of his designated area. He is not underfoot and he is not being fed all sorts of titbits that will probably cause him stomach distress, yet he still feels a part of the fun.

ESTABLISHING A TIMETABLE

A puppy should be taken to his relief area each time he is released from his designated area, after meals, after play sessions and when he first awakens in the morning (at age eight weeks, this can mean 5 a.m.!). The puppy will indicate that he's ready 'to go' by circling or sniffing busily—do not misinterpret these signs. For a puppy less than ten weeks of age, a routine of taking him out every hour is necessary. As the puppy grows, he will be able to wait for longer periods of time.

Keep trips to his relief area short. Stay no more than five or six minutes and then return to

HOW MANY TIMES A DAY?

AGE	RELIEF TRIPS
To 14 weeks	10
14–22 weeks	8
22–32 weeks	6
Adulthood	4
(dog stops growing)	

These are estimates, of course, but they are a guide to the *minimum* number of opportunities a dog should have each day to relieve himself.

the house. If he goes during that time, praise him lavishly and take him indoors immediately. If he does not, but he has an accident when you go back indoors, pick him up immediately, say 'No! No!' and return to his relief area. Wait a few minutes, then

Well-trained adults will be amenable to walking politely on lead, even with a child. This happy quartet is out enjoying a leisurely stroll.

return to the house again. Never hit a puppy or put his face in urine or excrement when he has had an accident!

Once indoors, put the puppy in his crate until you have had time to clean up his accident. Then release him to the family area and watch him more closely than before. Chances are, his accident was a result of your not picking up his signal or waiting too long before offering him the opportunity to relieve himself. Never hold a grudge against the puppy for accidents.

Let the puppy learn that going outdoors means it is time to relieve himself, not play. Once trained, he will be able to play indoors and out and still differentiate between the times for play versus the times for relief. Help him develop regular hours for naps, being alone, playing by himself and just resting, all in his crate. Encourage him to entertain himself while you are busy with your activities. Let him learn that having you near is comforting, but it is not your main purpose in life to provide him with undivided attention.

Each time you put your puppy in his own area, use the same command, whatever suits best. Soon he will run to his crate or special area when he hears you say those words. Crate training provides safety for you, the puppy and the home. It also provides the puppy with a feeling of security, and that helps the puppy achieve self-confidence and clean habits. Remember that one of the primary ingredients in house-training your puppy is control. Regardless of your

THE GOLDEN RULE

The golden rule of dog training is simple. For each 'question' (command), there is only one correct answer (reaction). One command = one reaction. Keep practising the command until the dog reacts correctly without hesitating. Be repetitive but not monotonous. Dogs get bored just as people do!

lifestyle, there will always be occasions when you will need to have a place where your dog can stay and be happy and safe. Crate training is the answer for now and in the future.

In conclusion, a few key elements are really all you need for a successful house-training method—consistency, frequency, praise, control and supervision. By following these procedures with a normal, healthy puppy, you and the puppy will soon be past the stage of 'accidents' and ready to move on to a clean and rewarding life together.

ROLES OF DISCIPLINE, REWARD AND PUNISHMENT

Discipline, training one to act in accordance with rules, brings order to life. It is as simple as that. Without discipline, particularly in a group society, chaos reigns supreme and the group will eventually perish. Humans and canines are social animals and need some form of discipline in order to function effectively. They must procure food, reproduce to keep the species going and protect their home base and their young. If there were no discipline in the lives of social animals, they would eventually die from starvation and/or predation by other stronger animals. In the case of domestic canines, dogs need discipline in their lives in order to understand how

their pack (you and other family members) functions and how they must act in order to survive.

A popular training philosophy centres around *Thorndike's Theory of Learning*, which states that a behaviour that results in a

PLAN TO PLAY
Your Manchester should also have regular play and exercise sessions when he is with you or a family member. Exercise for a very young puppy can consist of a short walk around the house or garden. Playing can include fetching games with a large ball or a special raggy. (All puppies teethe and need soft things upon which to chew.) Remember to restrict play periods to indoors within his living area (the family room, for example) until he is completely house-trained.

pleasant event tends to be repeated. Likewise, a behaviour that results in an unpleasant event tends not to be repeated. It is this theory on which training methods are based today. For example, if you manipulate a dog to perform a specific behaviour and reward him for doing it, he is likely to do it again because he enjoyed the end result.

Occasionally, punishment, a penalty inflicted for an offence, is necessary. The best type of punishment often comes from an outside source. For example, a child is told not to touch the cooker because he may get burned. He disobeys and touches

EASY DOES IT
Gently laying your hand over the top of the dog's neck right behind the ears acts as a dominant signal. Adding a soothing, soft voice with the word 'Easy' can calm an overly excited dog and help him resume a normal attitude.

the cooker. In doing so, he receives a burn. From that time on, he respects the heat of the cooker and avoids contact with it. Therefore, a behaviour that results in an unpleasant event tends not to be repeated.

A good example of a dog

A training lead, like this one, is made of strong nylon and slips easily over the dog's head. It provides control for the handler by tightening around the dog's neck as he pulls away from the handler.

learning the hard way is the dog who chases the house cat. He is told many times to leave the cat alone, yet he persists in teasing the cat. Then, one day he begins chasing the cat but the cat turns and swipes a claw across the dog's face, leaving him with a painful gash on his nose. The final result is that the dog stops chasing the cat.

TRAINING EQUIPMENT

COLLAR AND LEAD
For a Manchester, the collar and lead that you use for training must be one with which you are easily able to work, not too heavy for the dog and perfectly safe.

TREATS
Have a bag of treats on hand. Something nutritious and easy to swallow works best. Use a soft treat, a chunk of cheese or a piece of cooked chicken rather than a dry biscuit. By the time the dog has finished chewing a dry treat, he will forget why he is being rewarded in the first place! Bear in mind that using food rewards will not teach a dog to beg at the table—the only way to teach a dog to beg at the table is to give him food from the table. In training, rewarding the dog with a food treat will help him associate praise and the treats with learning new behaviours that obviously please his owner.

TRAINING RULES
If you want to be successful in training your dog, you have four rules to obey yourself:
1. Develop an understanding of how a dog thinks.
2. Do not blame the dog for lack of communication.
3. Define your dog's personality and act accordingly.
4. Have patience and be consistent.

TRAINING BEGINS: ASK THE DOG A QUESTION
In order to teach your dog anything, you must first get his attention. After all, he cannot learn anything if he is looking away from you with his mind on something else.

To get his attention, ask him 'School?' and immediately walk

Manchesters are among the most trainable of the terrier breeds. Look at the intensity with which this Manchester looks at his master, awaiting the next command.

toward the dog so that he must walk almost all the way to you. As he reaches you, give him the treat and praise again. By this time, the dog will probably be getting the idea that if he pays attention to you, especially when you ask that question, it will pay off in treats and enjoyable activities for him. In other words, he learns that 'school' means doing great things with you that are fun and result in positive attention for him.

over to him and give him a treat as you tell him 'Good dog.' Wait a minute or two and repeat the routine, this time with a treat in your hand as you approach within a foot of the dog. Do not go directly to him, but stop about a foot short of him and hold out the treat as you ask 'School?' He will see you approaching with a treat in your hand and most likely begin walking toward you. As you meet, give him the treat and praise again.

The third time, ask the question, have a treat in your hand and walk only a short distance

THE STUDENT'S STRESS TEST

During training sessions you must be able to recognise signs of stress in your dog such as:

- tucking his tail between his legs
- lowering his head
- shivering or trembling
- standing completely still or running away
- panting and/or salivating
- avoiding eye contact
- flattening his ears back
- urinating submissively
- rolling over and lifting a leg
- grinning or baring teeth
- aggression when restrained

If your four-legged student displays these signs, he may just be nervous or intimidated. The training session may have been too lengthy, with not enough praise and affirmation. Stop for the day and try again tomorrow.

The sit command makes an excellent starting point for every Manchester's education. If holding the treat above the dog's head doesn't convince him to sit, a little pressure on his bum likely will get him to sit.

DOUBLE JEOPARDY

A dog in jeopardy never lies down. He stays alert on his feet because instinct tells him that he may have to run away or fight for his survival. Therefore, if a dog feels threatened or anxious, he will not lie down. Consequently, it is important to keep the dog calm and relaxed as he learns the down exercise.

Remember that the dog does not understand your verbal language; he only recognises sounds. Your question translates to a series of sounds for him, and those sounds become the signal to go to you and pay attention; if he does, he will get to interact with you plus receive treats and praise.

BASIC OBEDIENCE COMMANDS

SIT COMMAND

Now that you have the dog's attention, attach his lead and hold it in your left hand and a food treat in your right. Place your food hand at the dog's nose and let him lick the treat but not take it from you. Say 'Sit' and slowly raise your food hand from in front of the dog's nose up over his head so that he is looking at the ceiling. As he bends his head upward, he will have to bend his knees to maintain his balance. As he bends his knees, he will assume a sit position. At that point, release the food treat and praise lavishly with comments such as 'Good dog! Good sit!' Remember to always praise enthusiastically, because dogs relish verbal praise from their owners and feel so proud of themselves whenever they accomplish a behaviour.

You will not use food forever in getting the dog to obey your commands. Food is only used to teach new behaviours, and once the dog knows what you want when you give a command, you will wean him off the food treats but still maintain the verbal praise. After all, you will always have your voice with you, and there will be many times when you have no food rewards but expect the dog to obey.

DOWN COMMAND

Teaching the down exercise is easy when you understand how the dog perceives the down position, and it is very difficult when you do not. Dogs perceive the down position as a submissive one; therefore, teaching the down exercise using a forceful method can sometimes make the dog develop such a fear of the down that he either runs away when you say 'Down' or he attempts to snap at the person who tries to force him down.

Have the dog sit close alongside your left leg, facing in the same direction as you are. Hold the lead in your left hand and a food treat in your right. Now place your left hand lightly on the top of the dog's shoulders where they meet above the spinal cord. Do not push down on the dog's shoulders; simply rest your left hand there so you can guide the dog to lie down close to your left leg rather than to swing away from your side when he drops.

Now place the food hand at the dog's nose, say 'Down' very softly (almost a whisper) and slowly lower the food hand to the dog's front feet. When the food hand reaches the floor, begin moving it forward along the floor in front of the dog. Keep talking softly to the dog, saying things like, 'Do you want this treat? You can do this, good dog.' Your reassuring tone of voice will

FEAR AGGRESSION

Pups who are subjected to physical abuse during training commonly end up with behavioural problems as adults. One common result of abuse is fear aggression, in which a dog will lash out, bare his teeth, snarl and finally bite someone by whom he feels threatened. For example, your daughter may be playing with the dog one afternoon. As they play hide-and-seek, she backs the dog into a corner and, as she attempts to tease him playfully, he bites her hand. Examine the cause of this behaviour. Did your daughter ever hit the dog? Did someone who resembles your daughter hit or scream at the dog?

Fortunately, fear aggression is relatively easy to correct. Have your daughter engage in only positive activities with the dog, such as feeding, petting and walking. She should not give any corrections or negative feedback. If the dog still growls or cowers away from her, allow someone else to accompany them. After approximately one week, the dog should feel that he can rely on her for many positive things, and he will also be prevented from reacting fearfully towards anyone who might resemble her.

help calm the dog as he tries to follow the food hand in order to get the treat.

When the dog's elbows touch the floor, release the food and praise softly. Try to get the dog to maintain that down position for several seconds before you let him sit up again. The goal here is to get the dog to settle down and not feel threatened in the down position.

Stay Command

It is easy to teach the dog to stay in either a sit or a down position. Again, we use food and praise during the teaching process as we help the dog to understand exactly what it is that we are

> **CONSISTENCY PAYS OFF**
> Dogs need consistency in their feeding times, exercise and toilet breaks, and in the verbal commands you use. If you use 'Stay' on Monday and 'Stay here, please' on Tuesday, you will confuse your dog. Don't demand perfect behaviour during training classes and then let him have the run of the house the rest of the day. Above all, lavish praise on your pet consistently every time he does something right. The more he feels he is pleasing you, the more willing he will be to learn.

expecting him to do. To teach the sit/stay, start with the dog sitting on your left side as before and hold the lead in your left hand. Have a food treat in your right hand and place your food hand at the dog's nose. Say 'Stay' and step out on your right foot to stand directly in front of the dog, toe to toe, as he licks and nibbles the treat. Be sure to keep his head facing upward to maintain the sit position. Count to five and then swing around to stand next to the dog again with him on your left. As soon as you get back to the original position, release the food and praise lavishly.

To teach the down/stay, do the down as previously described. As soon as the dog lies down, say 'Stay' and step out on your right foot just as you

Increase the distance between you and your Manchester as you practise the sit-stay. In time, the dog will obey from a considerable distance away from you.

did in the sit/stay. Count to five and then return to stand beside the dog with him on your left side. Release the treat and praise as always.

Within a week or ten days, you can begin to add a bit of distance between you and your dog when you leave him. When you do, use your left hand open with the palm facing the dog as a stay signal, much the same as the hand signal a constable uses to stop traffic at a crossroads. Hold the food treat in your right hand as before, but this time the food is not touching the dog's nose. He will watch the food hand and quickly learn that he is going to get that treat as soon as you return to his side.

When you can stand 1 metre away from your dog for 30 seconds, you can then begin building time and distance in both stays. Eventually, the dog

With practice, your Manchester Terrier will obey your commands off-lead and in any location. At first, practise the commands on-lead and in familiar locales free of distractions.

can be expected to remain in the stay position for prolonged periods of time until you return to him or call him to you. Always praise lavishly when he stays.

COME COMMAND

If you make teaching 'come' an exciting experience, you should never have a student that does not love the game or that fails to come when called. The secret, it seems, is never to teach the word 'come.'

At times when an owner most wants his dog to come when called, the owner is likely to be upset or anxious and he allows these feelings to come through in the tone of his voice when he calls his dog. Hearing

HELPING PAWS

Your dog may not be the next Lassie, but every pet has the potential to do some tricks well. Identify his natural talents and hone them. Is your dog always happy and upbeat? Teach him to wag his tail or give you his paw on command. Real homebodies can be trained to do household chores, such as carrying dirty washing or retrieving the morning paper.

'COME' . . . BACK

Never call your dog to come to you for a correction or scold him when he reaches you. That is the quickest way to turn a come command into 'Go away fast!' Dogs think only in the present tense, and your dog will connect the scolding with coming to you, not with the misbehaviour of a few moments earlier.

few food treats and each go into a different room in the house. Take turns calling the dog, and each person should celebrate the dog's finding him with a treat and lots of happy praise. When a person calls the dog, he is actually inviting the dog to find him and get a treat as a reward for 'winning.'

A few turns of the 'Where are you?' game and the dog will understand that everyone is playing the game and that each person has a big celebration awaiting his success at locating them. Once he learns to love the game, simply calling out 'Where are you?' will bring him running from wherever he is when he hears that all-important question.

The come command is recognised as one of the most important things to teach a dog, but there are trainers who work with thousands of dogs and never teach the actual word 'come.' Yet these dogs will race to respond to a person who uses the dog's name followed by 'Where are you?' For example, a woman has a 12-year-old companion dog who went blind, but who never fails to locate her owner when asked, 'Where are you?'

Children, in particular, love to play this game with their dogs. Children can hide in smaller places like a shower or bath, behind a bed or under a table. The dog needs to work a little bit harder to find these hiding places

that desperation in his owner's voice, the dog fears the results of going to him and therefore either disobeys outright or runs in the opposite direction. The secret, therefore, is to teach the dog a game and, when you want him to come to you, simply play the game. It is practically a no-fail solution!

To begin, have several members of your family take a

but, when he does, he really loves to celebrate with a treat and a tussle with a favourite youngster.

HEEL COMMAND

Heeling means that the dog walks beside the owner without pulling. It takes time and patience on the owner's part to succeed at teaching the dog that he (the owner) will not proceed unless the dog is walking calmly beside him. Pulling out ahead on the lead is definitely not acceptable.

Begin by holding the lead in your left hand as the dog sits beside your left leg. Move the loop end of the lead to your right hand but keep your left hand short on the lead so it keeps the dog in close next to you. Say 'Heel' and step forward on your left foot. Keep the dog close to you and take three steps. Stop and have the dog sit next to you

in what we now call the heel position. Praise verbally, but do not touch the dog. Hesitate a moment and begin again with 'Heel,' taking three steps and stopping, at which point the dog is told to sit again.

Your goal here is to have the dog walk those three steps without pulling on the lead. Once he will walk calmly beside you for three steps without pulling, increase the number of steps you take to five. When he will walk politely beside you while you take five steps, you can increase the length of your walk to ten steps. Keep increasing the length of your stroll until the dog will walk quietly beside you without

Only well-trained Manchesters could heel together with their mistress. If you own more than one Manchester, proper training is tantamount to maintaining your own sanity!

pulling as long as you want him to heel. When you stop heeling, indicate to the dog that the exercise is over by verbally praising as you pet him and say 'OK, good dog.' The 'OK' is used as a release word, meaning that the exercise is finished and the dog is free to relax.

If you are dealing with a dog who insists on pulling you around, simply 'put on your brakes' and stand your ground until the dog realises that the two of you are not going anywhere

until he is beside you and moving at your pace, not his. It may take some time just standing there to convince the dog that you are the leader and you will be the one to decide on the direction and speed of your travel.

Each time the dog looks up at you or slows down to give a slack lead between the two of you, quietly praise him and say, 'Good heel. Good dog.' Eventually, the dog will begin to respond and within a few days he will be walking politely beside you without pulling on the lead. At first, the training sessions should be kept short and very positive; soon the dog will be able to walk nicely with you for increasingly longer distances. Remember also to give the dog free time and the opportunity to run and play when you have finished heel practice.

WEANING OFF FOOD IN TRAINING
Food is used in training new behaviours. Once the dog

Heeling properly means that the dog walks politely at the pace set by the owner, making walks a pleasure for both!

understands what behaviour goes with a specific command, it is time to start weaning him off the food treats. At first, give a treat after each exercise. Then, start to give a treat only after every other exercise. Mix up the times when you offer a food reward and the times when you only offer praise so that the dog will never know when he is going to receive both food and praise and when he is going to receive only praise. This is called a variable-ratio reward system and it proves successful because there is always the chance that the owner will produce a treat, so the dog never stops trying for that reward. No matter what, *always* give verbal praise.

OBEDIENCE CLASSES

It is a good idea to enrol in an obedience class if one is available in your area. If yours is a show dog, ringcraft classes would be more appropriate. Many areas have dog clubs that offer basic obedience training as well as preparatory classes for obedience competition. There are also local dog trainers who offer similar classes.

At obedience shows, dogs can earn titles at various levels of competition. The beginning levels of competition include basic behaviours such as sit, down, heel and so on. The more advanced levels of competition

TUG OF WALK?
If you begin teaching the heel by taking long walks and letting the dog pull you along, he misinterprets this action as an acceptable form of taking a walk. When you pull back on the lead to counteract his pulling, he reads that tug as a signal to pull even harder!

include jumping, retrieving, scent discrimination and signal work. The advanced levels require a dog and owner to put a lot of time and effort into their training, and the titles that can be earned at these levels of competition are very prestigious.

OTHER ACTIVITIES FOR LIFE

Whether a dog is trained in the structured environment of a class or alone with his owner at home, there are many activities that can bring fun and rewards to both owner and dog once they have mastered basic control.

Teaching the dog to help out around the home, in the garden or on the farm provides great satisfaction to both dog and

Always praise your Manchester Terrier for a correct response to your command.

owner. In addition, the dog's help makes life a little easier for his owner and raises his stature as a valued companion to his family. It helps give the dog a purpose by occupying his mind and providing an outlet for his energy. The Manchester is not far removed from his working-dog ancestors, and he responds brilliantly as a farmhand and ratter. Give this a go, and you'll be delighted with the results.

Hiking is an exciting and healthy activity that the dog can be taught without assistance from more than his owner. The exercise of walking and climbing is good for man and dog alike, and the bond that they develop together is priceless.

If you are interested in participating in organised competition with your Manchester Terrier, there are activities other than obedience in

The rewards of a well-trained Manchester are long-lasting and worth every ounce of effort.

which you and your dog can become involved. Flyball has become very popular with Manchesters, and many all-breed clubs offer this activity. Likewise, agility is a popular sport where dogs run through an obstacle course that includes various jumps, tunnels and other exercises to test the dog's speed and coordination. The owners run beside their dogs to give commands and to guide them through the course. Although competitive, the focus is on fun—it's fun to do, fun to watch and great exercise.

NATURAL PRODIGY

Occasionally, a dog and owner who have not attended formal classes have been able to earn entry-level titles by obtaining competition rules and regulations from a local kennel club and practising on their own to a degree of perfection. Obtaining the higher level titles, however, almost always requires extensive training under the tutelage of experienced instructors. In addition, the more difficult levels require more specialised equipment whereas the lower levels do not.

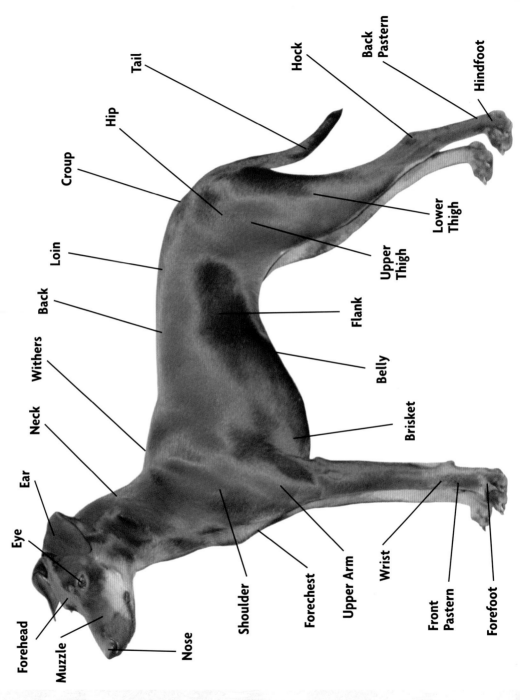

PHYSICAL STRUCTURE OF THE MANCHESTER TERRIER

Dogs suffer from many of the same physical illnesses as people. They might even share many of the same psychological problems. Since people usually know more about human diseases than canine maladies, many of the terms used in this chapter will be familiar but not necessarily those used by veterinary surgeons. We will use the term *x-ray*, instead of the more acceptable term *radiograph*. We will also use the familiar term *symptoms* even though dogs don't have symptoms, which are verbal descriptions of the patient's feelings; dogs have *clinical signs*. Since dogs can't speak, we have to look for *clinical signs*...but we still use the term *symptoms* in this book.

As a general rule, medicine is *practised*. That term is not arbitrary. Medicine is a constantly changing art as we learn more and more about genetics, electronic aids (like CAT scans and MRIs) and daily laboratory advances. There are many dog maladies, like canine hip dysplasia, which are not universally treated in the same manner. Some veterinary surgeons opt for surgery more often than others do.

SELECTING A VETERINARY SURGEON

Your selection of a veterinary surgeon should be based not only upon personality and ability with dogs, especially terriers, but also upon his convenience to your home. You want a vet who is close because you might have emergencies or need to make multiple visits for treatments. You want a vet who has services that you might require such as tattooing and boarding, as well as sophisticated pet supplies and a good reputation for ability and responsiveness. There is nothing more frustrating than having to wait a day or more to get a response from your veterinary surgeon.

All veterinary surgeons are licenced and their diplomas and/or certificates should be displayed in their waiting rooms. Most veterinary surgeons do routine surgery such as neutering, stitching up wounds and docking tails for those breeds in which such is required for show purposes. There are, however, many veterinary specialities that require further studies and internships. If needed, your vet will

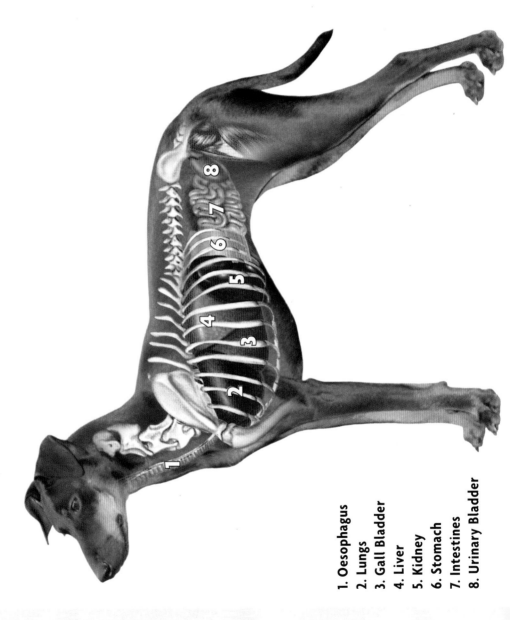

1. Oesophagus
2. Lungs
3. Gall Bladder
4. Liver
5. Kidney
6. Stomach
7. Intestines
8. Urinary Bladder

INTERNAL ORGANS OF THE MANCHESTER TERRIER

recommend a specialist at a nearby university school who is an expert in the relevant field, such as a veterinary cardiologist, dermatologist, ophthalmologist, etc.).

When the problem affecting your dog is serious, it is not unusual or impudent to get another medical opinion, although in Britain you are obliged to advise the vets concerned about this. You might also want to compare costs among several veterinary surgeons. Sophisticated health care and veterinary services can be very costly. It is not infrequent that important decisions are based upon financial considerations.

PREVENTATIVE MEDICINE

It is much easier, less costly and more effective to practise preventative medicine than to fight bouts of illness and disease. Properly bred puppies come from parents who were selected based upon their genetic-disease profiles. Their dam should have been vaccinated, free of all internal and external parasites and properly nourished. For these reasons, a visit to the veterinary surgeon who cared for the dam is recommended. The dam can pass on disease resistance to her puppies, which can last for eight to ten weeks. She can also pass on parasites and many infections. That's why you should learn as much about the dam's health as possible.

Breakdown of Veterinary Income by Category

2%	Dentistry
4%	Radiology
12%	Surgery
15%	Vaccinations
19%	Laboratory
23%	Examinations
25%	Medicines

A typical American vet's income, categorised according to services performed. This survey dealt with small-animal (pets) practices.

VACCINATION SCHEDULING
Most vaccinations are given by injection and should only be done by a veterinary surgeon. Both he and you should keep a record of the date of the injection, the identification of the vaccine and the amount given. Some vets give a first vaccination at eight weeks, but most dog breeders prefer the course not to commence until about ten weeks because of negating any antibodies passed on by the dam. The vaccination scheduling is usually based on a 15-day cycle. You must take your vet's advice regarding when to vaccinate, as this may differ according to the vaccine used.

Most vaccinations immunise your puppy against viruses. The usual vaccines contain immunising doses of several different viruses such as distemper, parvovirus, parainfluenza and

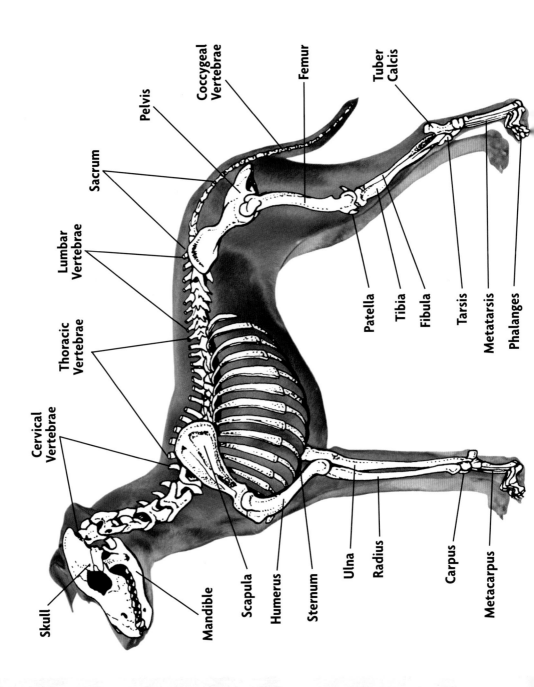

Coccygeal
Vertebrae

Pelvis

Femur

Tuber
Calcis

Sacrum

Lumbar
Vertebrae

Patella

Tibia

Fibula

Tarsis

Metatarsis

Phalanges

Thoracic
Vertebrae

Cervical
Vertebrae

Skull

Mandible

Scapula

Humerus

Sternum

Ulna

Radius

Carpus

Metacarpus

SKELETAL STRUCTURE OF THE MANCHESTER TERRIER

hepatitis although some veterinary surgeons recommend separate vaccines for each disease. There are other vaccines available when the puppy is at risk. You should rely upon professional advice. This is especially true for the booster-shot programme. Most vaccination programmes require a booster when the puppy is a year old and once a year thereafter. In some cases, circumstances may require more or less frequent immunizations. Canine cough, more formally known as tracheobronchitis, is treated with a vaccine that is sprayed into the dog's nostrils. Canine cough is usually included in routine vaccination, but this is often not as effective as the vaccines for other major diseases.

WEANING TO FIVE MONTHS OLD

Puppies should be weaned by the time they are about two months old. A puppy that remains for at least eight weeks with his dam and littermates usually adapts better to other dogs and people later in life.

Sometimes new owners have their puppy examined by a veterinary surgeon immediately, which is a good idea. Vaccination programmes usually begin when the puppy is very young.

The puppy will have his teeth examined and have his skeletal conformation and general health checked prior to certification by the veterinary surgeon. Puppies in certain breeds have problems with their kneecaps, cataracts and other eye problems, heart murmurs and undescended testicles. They may also have personality problems and your vet might have training in temperament evaluation.

FIVE TO TWELVE MONTHS OF AGE

Unless you intend to breed or show your dog, neutering the puppy at six months of age is recommended. Discuss this with your veterinary surgeon. Neutering has proven to be extremely beneficial to both male and female dogs. Besides eliminating the possibility of pregnancy and pyometra in bitches and testicular cancer in male dogs, it greatly reduces the risk of (but does not prevent) breast cancer in bitches and prostate cancer in male dogs.

Your veterinary surgeon should provide your puppy with a thorough dental evaluation at six months of age, ascertaining whether all of the permanent teeth have erupted properly. A home dental-care regimen should be initiated at six months, including brushing weekly and providing good dental devices (such as nylon bones). Regular dental care promotes healthy teeth, fresh breath and a longer life.

Normal hairs of a dog, enlarged 200 times original size. The cuticle (outer covering) is clean and healthy. Unlike human hair that grows from the base, a dog's hair also grows from the end. Damaged hairs and split ends, illustrated above.

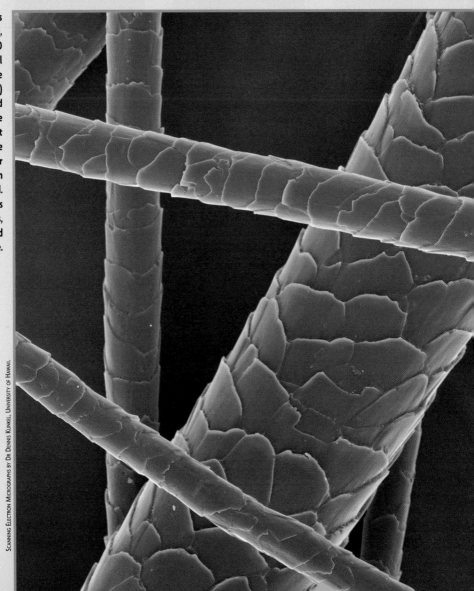

HEALTH AND VACCINATION TIMETABLE

AGE IN WEEKS:	6TH	8TH	10TH	12TH	14TH	16TH	20-24TH	52ND
Worm Control	✔	✔	✔	✔	✔	✔	✔	
Neutering							✔	
Heartworm		✔		✔		✔	✔	
Parvovirus			✔		✔		✔	✔
Distemper		✔		✔		✔		✔
Hepatitis		✔		✔		✔		✔
Leptospirosis								✔
Parainfluenza			✔		✔			✔
Dental Examination		✔					✔	✔
Complete Physical		✔					✔	✔
Coronavirus				✔			✔	✔
Canine Cough								
Hip Dysplasia							✔	
Rabies							✔	

Vaccinations are not instantly effective. It takes about two weeks for the dog's immune system to develop antibodies. Most vaccinations require annual booster shots. Your veterinary surgeon should guide you in this regard.

OVER ONE YEAR OF AGE

Once a year, your fully-grown dog should visit the vet for an examination and vaccination boosters, if needed. Some vets recommend blood tests, thyroid level check and dental evaluation to accompany these annual visits. A thorough clinical evaluation by the vet can provide critical background information for your dog. Blood tests are often performed at one year of age, and dental examinations should be part of routine check-ups. In the long run, quality preventative care for your pet can save money, teeth and lives.

SKIN PROBLEMS IN MANCHESTER TERRIERS

Veterinary surgeons are consulted by dog owners for skin problems more than for any other group of diseases or maladies. Dogs' skin is almost as sensitive as human skin and both can suffer from almost the same ailments (though the occurrence of acne in most dogs is rare). For this reason, veterinary dermatology has developed into a speciality practised by many veterinary surgeons.

Since many skin problems have visual symptoms that are almost identical, it requires the

DISEASE REFERENCE CHART

	What is it?	What causes it?	Symptoms
Leptospirosis	Severe disease that affects the internal organs; can be spread to people.	A bacterium, which is often carried by rodents, that enters through mucous membranes and spreads quickly throughout the body.	Range from fever, vomiting and loss of appetite in less severe cases to shock, irreversible kidney damage and possibly death in most severe cases.
Rabies	Potentially deadly virus that infects warm-blooded mammals. Not seen in United Kingdom.	Bite from a carrier of the virus, mainly wild animals.	1st stage: dog exhibits change in behaviour, fear. 2nd stage: dog's behaviour becomes more aggressive. 3rd stage: loss of coordination, trouble with bodily functions.
Parvovirus	Highly contagious virus, potentially deadly.	Ingestion of the virus, which is usually spread through the faeces of infected dogs.	Most common: severe diarrhoea. Also vomiting, fatigue, lack of appetite.
Canine cough	Contagious respiratory infection.	Combination of types of bacteria and virus. Most common: *Bordetella bronchiseptica* bacteria and parainfluenza virus.	Chronic cough.
Distemper	Disease primarily affecting respiratory and nervous system.	Virus that is related to the human measles virus.	Mild symptoms such as fever, lack of appetite and mucous secretion progress to evidence of brain damage, 'hard pad.'
Hepatitis	Virus primarily affecting the liver.	Canine adenovirus type I (CAV-1). Enters system when dog breathes in particles.	Lesser symptoms include listlessness, diarrhoea, vomiting. More severe symptoms include 'blue-eye' (clumps of virus in eye).
Coronavirus	Virus resulting in digestive problems.	Virus is spread through infected dog's faeces.	Stomach upset evidenced by lack of appetite, vomiting, diarrhoea.

skill of an experienced veterinary dermatologist to identify and cure many of the more severe skin disorders. Pet shops sell many treatments for skin problems but most of the treatments are directed at symptoms and not the underlying problem(s). If your dog is suffering from a skin disorder, you should seek professional assistance as quickly as possible. As with all diseases, the earlier a problem is identified and treated, the more successful is the cure.

HEREDITARY SKIN DISORDERS
Veterinary dermatologists are currently researching a number of skin disorders that are believed to have hereditary bases. These inherited diseases are transmitted by both parents, who appear (phenotypically) normal but have a recessive gene for the disease, meaning that they carry, but are not affected by, the disease. These diseases pose serious problems to breeders because in some instances there is no method of identifying carriers. Often the secondary diseases associated with these skin conditions are even more debilitating than the disorder itself, including cancers and respiratory problems.

Among the hereditary skin disorders, for which the mode of inheritance is known, are acrodermatitis, cutaneous asthenia (Ehlers-Danlos syndrome), sebaceous adenitis, cyclic hematopoiesis, dermatomyositis, IgA deficiency, colour dilution alopaecia and nodular dermatofibrosis. Some of these disorders are limited to one or two breeds and others affect a large number of breeds. All inherited diseases must be diagnosed and treated by a veterinary specialist.

PARASITE BITES

Many of us are allergic to insect bites. The bites itch, erupt and may even become infected. Dogs have the same reaction to fleas, ticks and/or mites. When an insect lands on you, you have the chance to whisk it away with your hand. Unfortunately, when your dog is bitten by a flea, tick or mite, he can only scratch it away or bite it. By the time the dog has been bitten, the parasite has done some of its damage. It may also have laid eggs to cause further problems in the near future. The itching from parasite bites is probably due to the saliva injected into the site when the parasite sucks the dog's blood.

AUTO-IMMUNE SKIN CONDITIONS

Auto-immune skin conditions are commonly referred to as being allergic to yourself, while allergies are usually inflammatory reactions to an outside stimulus. Auto-immune diseases cause serious damage to the tissues that are involved.

The best known auto-immune disease is lupus, which affects people as well as dogs. The symptoms are variable and may affect the kidneys, bones, blood chemistry and skin. It can be fatal to both dogs and humans, though it is not thought to be transmissible. It is usually successfully treated with cortisone, prednisone or a similar corticosteroid, but extensive use of these drugs can have harmful side effects.

AIRBORNE ALLERGIES

Just as humans have hay fever, rose fever and other allergies from which they suffer during the pollinating season, many dogs suffer from the same allergies. When the pollen count is high, your dog might suffer but don't expect him to sneeze and have a runny nose as a human would. Dogs react to pollen allergies the same way they react to fleas—they scratch and bite themselves.

Dogs, like humans, can be tested for allergens. Discuss the testing with your veterinary dermatologist.

FOOD PROBLEMS

FOOD ALLERGIES

Dogs can be allergic to many foods that are best-sellers and highly recommended by breeders and veterinary surgeons.

Changing the brand of food that you buy may not eliminate the problem if the element to which the dog is allergic is contained in the new brand.

Recognising a food allergy is difficult. Humans vomit or have rashes when they eat a food to which they are allergic. Dogs neither vomit nor (usually) develop a rash. They react in the same manner as they do to an airborne or flea allergy; they itch, scratch and bite, thus making the diagnosis extremely difficult. While pollen allergies and parasite bites are usually seasonal, food allergies are year-round problems.

FOOD INTOLERANCE

Food intolerance is the inability of the dog to completely digest certain foods. For example, puppies that may have done very well on their dam's milk may not do well on cow's milk. The result of this food intolerance may be loose bowels, passing gas and stomach pains. These are the only obvious symptoms of food intolerance and that makes diagnosis difficult.

TREATING FOOD PROBLEMS

It is possible to handle food allergies and food intolerance yourself. Put your dog on a diet that he has never had. Obviously, if he has never eaten this new food, he can't yet have been allergic or intolerant of it. Start with a single ingredient that is not in the dog's diet at the present time. Ingredients like chopped beef or chicken are common in dogs' diets, so try something different like rabbit, fish, lamb or any other quality source of animal protein. Keep the dog on this diet (with no additives) for a month. If the symptoms of food allergy or intolerance disappear, chances are your dog has a food allergy.

Don't think that the single ingredient cured the problem. You still must find a suitable diet and ascertain which ingredient in the old diet was objectionable. This is most easily done by adding ingredients to the new diet one at a time. Let the dog stay on the modified diet for a month before you add another ingredient. Eventually, you will determine the ingredient that caused the adverse reaction.

An alternative method is to carefully study the ingredients in the diet to which your dog is allergic or intolerant. Identify the main ingredient in this diet and eliminate the main ingredient by buying a different food that does not have that ingredient. Keep experimenting until the symptoms disappear after one month on the new diet.

Recognising a Sick Dog

Unlike colicky babies and cranky children, our canine charges cannot tell us when they are feeling ill. Therefore, there are a number of signs that owners can identify to know that their dogs are not feeling well.

Take note for physical manifestations such as:

- unusual, bad odour, including bad breath
- excessive moulting
- wax in the ears, chronic ear irritation
- oily, flaky, dull haircoat
- mucous, tearing or similar discharge in the eyes
- fleas or mites
- mucous in stool, diarrhoea
- sensitivity to petting or handling
- licking at paws, scratching face, etc.

Keep an eye out for behavioural changes as well, including:

- lethargy, idleness
- lack of patience or general irritability
- lack of appetite
- phobias (fear of people, loud noises, etc.)
- strange behaviour, suspicion, fear
- coprophagia
- more frequent barking
- whimpering, crying

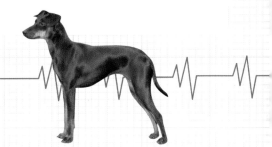

Get Well Soon

You don't need a DVR or a BVMA to provide good TLC to your sick or recovering dog, but you do need to pay attention to some details that normally wouldn't bother him. The following tips will aid Fido's recovery and get him back on his paws again:

- Keep his space free of irritating smells, like heavy perfumes and air fresheners.
- Rest is the best medicine! Avoid harsh lighting that will prevent your dog from sleeping. Shade him from bright sunlight during the day and dim the lights in the evening.
- Keep the noise level down. Animals are more sensitive to sound when they are sick.

- Be attentive to any necessary temperature adjustments. A dog with a fever needs a cool room and cold liquids. A bitch that is whelping or recovering from surgery will be more comfortable in a warm room, consuming warm liquids and food.
- You wouldn't send a sick child back to school early, so don't rush your dog back into a full routine until he seems absolutely ready.

A male dog flea, *Ctenocephalides canis.*

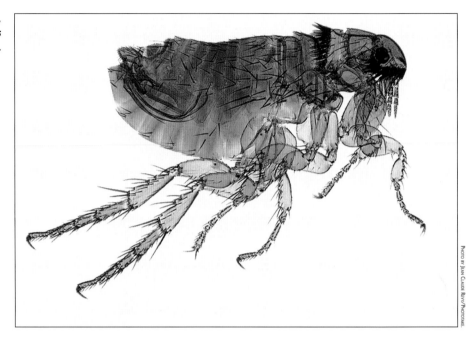

Photo by Jean Claude Revy/Phototake

EXTERNAL PARASITES

FLEAS

Of all the problems to which dogs are prone, none is more well known and frustrating than fleas. Flea infestation is relatively simple to cure but difficult to prevent. Parasites that are harboured inside the body are a bit more difficult to eradicate but they are easier to control.

To control flea infestation, you have to understand the flea's life cycle. Fleas are often thought of as a summertime problem, but centrally heated homes have changed the patterns and fleas can be found at any time of the year. The most effective method of flea control is a two-stage approach: one stage to kill the adult fleas, and the other to control the development of pre-adult fleas. Unfortunately, no single active ingredient is effective against all stages of the life cycle.

FLEA KILLER CAUTION— 'POISON'

Flea-killers are poisonous. You should not spray these toxic chemicals on areas of a dog's body that he licks, including his genitals and his face. Flea killers taken internally are a better answer, but check with your veterinary surgeon in case internal therapy is not advised for your dog.

LIFE CYCLE STAGES

During its life, a flea will pass through four life stages: egg, larva, pupa or nymph and adult. The adult stage is the most visible and irritating stage of the flea life cycle, and this is why the majority of flea-control products concentrate on this stage. The fact is that adult fleas account for only 1% of the total flea population, and the other 99% exist in pre-adult stages, i.e. eggs, larvae and nymphs. The pre-adult stages are barely visible to the naked eye.

THE LIFE CYCLE OF THE FLEA

Eggs are laid on the dog, usually in quantities of about 20 or 30, several times a day. The adult female flea must have a blood meal before each egg-laying session. When first laid, the eggs will cling to the dog's hair, as the eggs are still moist. However, they will quickly dry out and fall from the dog, especially if the dog moves around or scratches. Many eggs will fall off in the dog's favourite area or an area in which he spends a lot of time, such as his bed.

Once the eggs fall from the dog onto the carpet or furniture, they will hatch into larvae. This takes from one to ten days. Larvae are not particularly mobile and will usually travel only a few inches from where they hatch. However, they do have a tendency to move away from

EN GARDE:
CATCHING FLEAS OFF GUARD!
Consider the following ways to arm yourself against fleas:
- Add a small amount of pennyroyal or eucalyptus oil to your dog's bath. These natural remedies repel fleas.
- Supplement your dog's food with fresh garlic (minced or grated) and an hearty amount of brewer's yeast, both of which ward off fleas.
- Use a flea comb on your dog daily. Submerge fleas in a cup of bleach to kill them quickly.
- Confine the dog to only a few rooms to limit the spread of fleas in the home.
- Vacuum daily . . . and get all of the crevices! Dispose of the bag every few days until the problem is under control.
- Wash your dog's bedding daily. Cover cushions where your dog sleeps with towels, and wash the towels often.

bright light and heavy traffic—under furniture and behind doors are common places to find high quantities of flea larvae.

The flea larvae feed on dead organic matter, including adult flea faeces, until they are ready to change into adult fleas. Fleas will usually remain as larvae for around seven days. After this period, the larvae will pupate into protective pupae. While inside the pupae, the larvae will undergo

Fleas have been measured as being able to jump 300,000 times and can jump over 150 times their length in any direction, including straight up.

metamorphosis and change into adult fleas. This can take as little time as a few days, but the adult fleas can remain inside the pupae waiting to hatch for up to two years. The pupae are signalled to hatch by certain stimuli, such as physical pressure—the pupae's being stepped on, heat from an animal's lying on the pupae or increased carbon-dioxide levels and vibrations—indicating that a suitable host is available.

Once hatched, the adult flea must feed within a few days. Once the adult flea finds an host, it will not leave voluntarily. It only becomes dislodged by grooming or the host animal's scratching. The adult flea will

remain on the host for the duration of its life unless forcibly removed.

TREATING THE ENVIRONMENT AND THE DOG

Treating fleas should be a two-pronged attack. First, the environment needs to be treated; this includes carpets and furniture, especially the dog's bedding and areas underneath furniture. The environment should be treated with an household spray containing an Insect Growth Regulator (IGR) and an insecticide to kill the adult fleas. Most IGRs are effective against eggs and larvae; they actually mimic the fleas' own hormones and stop the eggs and larvae from developing into adult fleas. There are currently no treatments available to attack the pupa stage of the life cycle, so the adult insecticide is used to kill the newly hatched adult fleas before they find an host. Most IGRs are active for many months, while adult insecticides are only

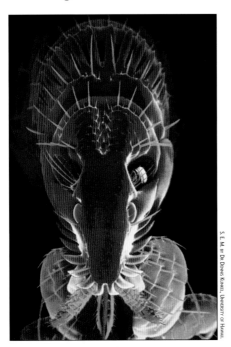

A scanning electron micrograph of a dog or cat flea, *Ctenocephalides*, magnified more than 100x. This image has been colourised for effect.

THE LIFE CYCLE OF THE FLEA

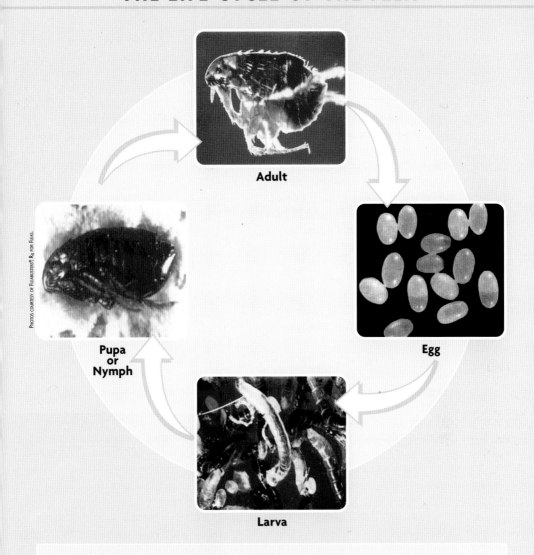

Adult

Egg

Larva

Pupa
or
Nymph

Fleas have been around for millions of years and have adapted to changing host animals. They are able to go through a complete life cycle in less than one month or they can extend their lives to almost two years by remaining as pupae or cocoons. They do not need blood or any other food for up to 20 months.

INSECT GROWTH REGULATOR (IGR)

Two types of products should be used when treating fleas—a product to treat the pet and a product to treat the home. Adult fleas represent less than 1% of the flea population. The pre-adult fleas (eggs, larvae and pupae) represent more than 99% of the flea population and are found in the environment; it is in the case of pre-adult fleas that products containing an Insect Growth Regulator (IGR) should be used in the home.

IGRs are a new class of compound used to prevent the development of insects. They do not kill the insect outright; instead, they use the insect's biology against it to stop it from completing its growth. Products that contain methoprene are the world's first and leading IGRs. Used to control fleas and other insects, this type of IGR will stop flea larvae from developing and protect the house for up to seven months.

The American dog tick, *Dermacentor variabilis*, is probably the most common tick found on dogs. Look at the strength in its eight legs! No wonder it's hard to detach them.

active for a few days.

When treating with an household spray, it is a good idea to vacuum before applying the product. This stimulates as many pupae as possible to hatch into adult fleas. The vacuum cleaner should also be treated with an insecticide to prevent the eggs and larvae that have been hoovered in the vacuum bag from hatching.

The second stage of treatment is to apply an adult insecticide to the dog. Traditionally, this would be in the form of a collar or a spray, but more recent innovations include digestible insecticides that poison the fleas when they ingest the dog's blood. Alternatively, there are drops that, when placed on the back of the dog's neck, spread throughout the hair and skin to kill adult fleas.

TICKS

Though not as common as fleas, ticks are found all over the tropical and temperate world. They don't bite, like fleas; they harpoon. They dig their sharp proboscis (nose) into the dog's skin and drink the blood. Their only food and drink is dog's

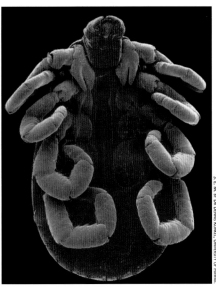

S. E. M. BY DR DENNIS KUNKEL, UNIVERSITY OF HAWAII

blood. Dogs can get Lyme disease, Rocky Mountain spotted fever (normally found in the US only), tick bite paralysis and many other diseases from ticks. They may live where fleas are found and they like to hide in cracks or seams in walls. They are controlled the same way fleas are controlled.

The American dog tick, *Dermacentor variabilis*, may well be the most common dog tick in many geographical areas, especially those areas where the climate is hot and humid. Most dog ticks have life expectancies of a week to six months, depending upon climatic conditions. They can neither jump nor fly, but they can crawl slowly and can range up to 5 metres (16 feet) to reach a sleeping or unsuspecting dog.

MITES

Just as fleas and ticks can be problematic for your dog, mites can also lead to an itchy nuisance. Microscopic in size, mites are related to ticks and generally take up permanent residence on their host animal—in this case, your dog! The term *mange* refers to any infestation caused by one of the mighty mites, of which there are six varieties that concern dog owners.

Demodex mites cause a condition known as demodicosis (sometimes called red mange or follicular mange), in which the

DEER-TICK CROSSING
The great outdoors may be fun for your dog, but it also is home to dangerous ticks. Deer ticks carry a bacterium known as *Borrelia burgdorferi* and are most active in the autumn and spring. When infections are caught early, penicillin and tetracycline are effective antibiotics, but, if left untreated, the bacteria may cause neurological, kidney and cardiac problems as well as long-term trouble with walking and painful joints.

S. E. M. BY DR ANDREW SPIELMAN/PHOTOTAKE.

PHOTO BY DR. DENNIS KUNKEL, UNIVERSITY OF HAWAII.

The head of an American dog tick, *Dermacentor variabilis*, enlarged and colourised for effect.

PHOTO BY JAMES HAYDEN/YOAV/PHOTOTAKE.

mites live in the dog's hair folli-
cles and sebaceous glands in
larger-than-normal
numbers. This type of
mange is
commonly passed
from the dam to
her puppies and
usually shows up
on the puppies'
muzzles, though
demodicosis is
not transferable
from one normal dog to
another. Most dogs recover from
this type of mange without any
treatment, though topical thera-
pies are commonly prescribed by
the vet.

The *Cheyletiellosis* mite is the
hook-mouthed culprit associated

with 'walking dandruff,' a condition that affects dogs as well as
cats and rabbits. This mite lives
on the surface of the animal's skin
and is readily transferable
through direct or indirect contact
with an affected animal. The
dandruff is present in the form of
scaly skin, which may or may not
be itchy. If not treated, this mange
can affect a whole kennel of dogs
and can be spread to humans as
well.

The *Sarcoptes* mite causes
intense itching on the dog in the
form of a condition known as
scabies or sarcoptic mange. The
cycle of the *Sarcoptes* mite lasts
about three weeks, and the mites
live in the top layer of the dog's
skin (epidermis), preferably in

areas with little hair. Scabies is highly contagious and can be passed to humans. Sometimes an allergic reaction to the mite worsens the severe itching associated with sarcoptic mange.

Ear mites, *Otodectes cynotis,* lead to otodectic mange, which most commonly affects the outer ear canal of the dog, though other areas can be affected as well. Dogs with ear-mite infestation commonly scratch at their ears, causing further irritation, and shake their heads. Dark brown droppings in the outer ear confirm the diagnosis. Your vet can prescribe a treatment to flush out the ears and kill any eggs in the ears. A complete month of treatment is necessary to cure the mange.

Two other mites, less common in dogs, include *Dermanyssus gallinae* (the poultry or red mite) and *Eutrombicula alfreddugesi* (the mite associated with trombiculidiasis or chigger infestation). The poultry mite frequently lives on chickens, but can transfer to dogs who spend time near farm animals. Chigger infestation affects dogs who have exposure to

NOT A DROP TO DRINK
Never allow your dog to swim in polluted water or public areas where water quality can be suspect. Even perfectly clear water can harbour parasites, many of which can cause serious to fatal illnesses in canines. Areas inhabited by waterfowl and other wildlife are especially dangerous.

woodlands. The types of mange caused by both of these mites are treatable by vets.

INTERNAL PARASITES
Most animals—fishes, birds and mammals, including dogs and humans—have worms and other parasites that live inside their bodies. According to Dr Herbert R Axelrod, the fish pathologist, there are two kinds of parasites: dumb and smart. The smart parasites live in peaceful cooperation with their hosts (symbiosis), while the dumb parasites kill their hosts. Most worm infections are relatively easy to control. If they are not controlled, they weaken the host dog to the point that other medical problems occur, but they do not kill the host as dumb parasites would.

A brown dog tick, *Rhipicephalus sanguineus,* is an uncommon but annoying tick found on dogs.
PHOTO BY CAROLINA BIOLOGICAL SUPPLY/PHOTOTAKE.

DO NOT MIX
Never mix flea-control products without first consulting your veterinary surgeon. Some products can become toxic when combined with others and can cause serious or fatal consequences.

Photo by Carolina Biological Supply/Phototake

The roundworm *Rhabditis* can infect both dogs and humans.

The roundworm, *Ascaris lumbricoides.*

ROUNDWORMS

Average-size dogs can pass 1,360,000 roundworm eggs every day. For example, if there were only 1 million dogs in the world, the world would be saturated with 1,300 metric tonnes of dog faeces. These faeces would contain 15,000,000,000 roundworm eggs.

7–31% of home gardens and children's play boxes in the US contain roundworm eggs.

Flushing dog's faeces down the toilet is not a safe practice because the usual sewage treatments do not destroy roundworm eggs.

Infected puppies start shedding roundworm eggs at three weeks of age. They can be infected by their mother's milk.

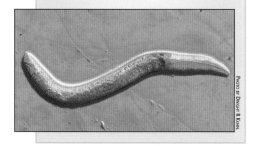

Photo by Dwight R Kuhn.

ROUNDWORMS

The roundworms that infect dogs are known scientifically as *Toxocara canis.* They live in the dog's intestines and shed eggs continually. It has been estimated that a dog produces about 150 grammes of faeces every day. Each gramme of faeces averages 10,000–12,000 eggs of roundworm. There are no known areas in which dogs roam that do not contain roundworm eggs. The greatest danger of roundworms is that they infect people, too! It is wise to have your dog tested regularly for roundworms.

In young puppies, roundworms cause bloated bellies, diarrhoea, coughing and vomiting, and are transmitted from the dam (through blood or milk). Affected puppies will not appear as animated as normal puppies. The worms appear spaghetti-like, measuring as long as 15 cms (6 inches). Adult dogs can acquire roundworms through coprophagia (eating contaminated faeces) or by killing rodents that carry roundworms.

Roundworm infection can kill puppies and cause severe problems in adults, as the hatched larvae travel to the lungs and trachea through the bloodstream. Cleanliness is the best preventative for roundworms. Always pick up after your dog and dispose of faeces in appropriate receptacles.

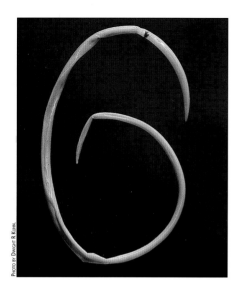

HOOKWORMS

Dog owners have to be concerned about four different species of hookworm, the most common and most serious of which is *Ancylostoma caninum,* which prefers warm climates. The others are *Ancylostoma braziliense, Ancylostoma tubaeforme* and *Uncinaria stenocephala,* the latter of which is a concern to dogs living in cold climates. Hookworms are dangerous to humans as well as to dogs and cats, and can be the cause of severe anaemia due to iron deficiency. The worm uses its teeth to attach itself to the dog's intestines and changes the site of its attachment about six times per day. Each time the worm repositions itself, the dog loses blood and can become anaemic. *Ancylostoma caninum* is the most likely of the four species to cause anaemia in the dog.

Symptoms of hookworm infection include dark stools, weight loss, general weakness, pale coloration and anaemia, as well as possible skin problems. Fortunately, hookworms are easily purged from the affected dog with a number of medications that have proven effective. Discuss these with your vet. Most heartworm preventatives include a hookworm insecticide as well.

Owners also must be aware that hookworms can infect humans, who can acquire the larvae through exposure to contaminated faeces. Since the worms cannot complete their life cycle on a human, the worms simply infest the skin and cause irritation. This condition is known as cutaneous larva migrans syndrome. As a preventative, use disposable gloves or a 'poop-scoop' to pick up your dog's droppings and prevent your dog (or neighbourhood cats) from defecating in children's play areas.

In Britain the 'temperate climate' hookworm (*Uncinaria stenocephala*) is rarely found in

The hookworm, *Ancylostoma caninum.*

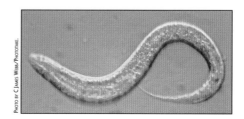

The infective stage of the hookworm larva.

TAPEWORMS

Humans, rats, squirrels, foxes, coyotes, wolves and domestic dogs are all susceptible to tapeworm infection. Except in humans, tapeworms are usually not a fatal infection. Infected individuals can harbour 1000 parasitic worms.

Tapeworms, like some other types of worm, are hermaphroditic, meaning male and female in the same worm.

If dogs eat infected rats or mice, or anything else infected with tapeworm, they get the tapeworm disease. One month after attaching to a dog's intestine, the worm starts shedding eggs. These eggs are infective immediately. Infective eggs can live for a few months without a host animal.

flea that is carrying tapeworm eggs.

While tapeworm infection is not life-threatening in dogs (smart parasite!), it can be the cause of a very serious liver disease for humans. About 50% of the humans infected with *Echinococcus multilocularis*, a type of tapeworm that causes alveolar hydatid, perish.

WHIPWORMS

Whipworms are counted among the most common parasitic worms in dogs. The whipworm's scientific name is *Trichuris vulpis*. These worms attach themselves in the lower parts of the intestine, where they feed. Affected dogs may only experience upset tummies, colic and diarrhoea. These worms, however, can live for months or years in the dog, beginning their larval stage in the small intestine, spending their adult stage in the large intestine and finally passing infective eggs through the dog's faeces.

pet or show dogs, but can occur in hunting packs, racing Greyhounds and sheepdogs because the worms can be prevalent wherever dogs are exercised regularly on grassland.

TAPEWORMS

The head and rostellum (the round prominence on the scolex) of a tapeworm, which infects dogs and humans.

There are many species of tapeworm, all of which are carried by fleas! The most common tapeworm affecting dogs is known as *Dipylidium caninum*. The dog eats the flea and starts the tapeworm cycle. Humans can also be infected with tapeworms—so don't eat fleas! Fleas are so small that your dog could pass them onto your hands, your plate or your food and thus make it possible for you to ingest a

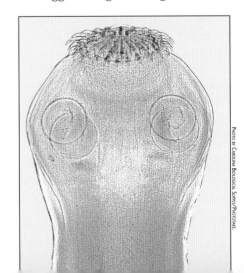

The only way to detect whipworms is through a faecal examination, though this is not always foolproof. Treatment for whipworms is tricky, due to the worms' unusual life-cycle pattern, and very often dogs are reinfected due to exposure to infective eggs on the ground. The whipworm eggs can survive in the environment for as long as five years; thus, cleaning up droppings in your own garden as well as in public places is absolutely essential for sanitation purposes and the health of your dog and others.

THREADWORMS
Though less common than round-worms, hookworms and those previously mentioned, thread-worms concern dog owners in areas where the climate is hot and humid. Living in the small intes-tine of the dog, this worm measures a mere 2 millimetres and is round in shape. Like that of the whip-worm, the threadworm's life cycle is very complex and the eggs and larvae are passed through the faeces. A deadly disease in humans, *Strongyloides* readily infects people, and the handling of faeces is the most common means of transmission. Threadworms are most often seen in young puppies; bloody diarrhoea and pneumonia are symptoms. Sick puppies must be isolated and treated immedi-ately; vets recommend a follow-up treatment one month later.

HEARTWORM PREVENTATIVES

With the dawn of relaxed quarantine regula-tions, heartworm preventatives are being introduced on the market. Some of these heartworm preventatives may be sold at your veterinary surgeon's office. These prod-ucts can be given daily or monthly, depend-ing on the manufacturer's instructions. All of these preventatives contain chemical insec-ticides directed at killing heartworms, which leads to some controversy among dog owners. In effect, heartworm preventatives are necessary evils, though you should determine how necessary based on your pet's lifestyle. There is no doubt that heart-worm is a dreadful disease that threatens the lives of dogs. However, the likelihood of your dog's being bitten by an infected mosquito is slim in most places, and a mosquito-repellent (or an herbal remedy such as Wormwood or Black Walnut) is much safer for your dog and will not compromise his immune system (the way heartworm preventatives will). Should you decide to use the traditional preventative 'medications,' you can consider giving the pill every other or third month. Since the toxins in the pill will kill the heartworms at all stages of development, the pill would be effective in killing larvae, nymphs or adults, and it takes four months for the larvae to reach the adult stage. Thus, there is no rationale to poisoning the dog's system on a monthly basis. Lastly, do not give the pill during the winter months, since there are no mosquitoes around to pass on their infec-tion.

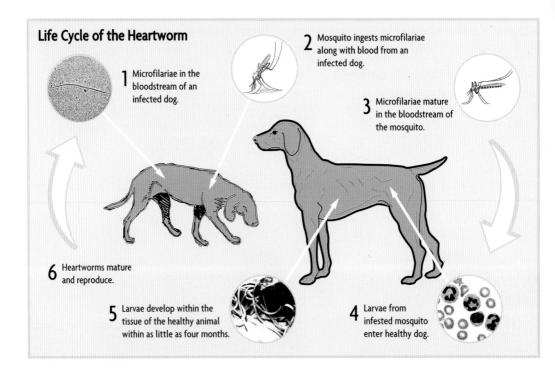

Life Cycle of the Heartworm

1 Microfilariae in the bloodstream of an infected dog.

2 Mosquito ingests microfilariae along with blood from an infected dog.

3 Microfilariae mature in the bloodstream of the mosquito.

6 Heartworms mature and reproduce.

5 Larvae develop within the tissue of the healthy animal within as little as four months.

4 Larvae from infested mosquito enter healthy dog.

HEARTWORMS

Heartworms are thin, extended worms up to 30 cms (12 inches) long, which live in a dog's heart and the major blood vessels surrounding it. Dogs may have up to 200 worms. Symptoms may be loss of energy, loss of appetite, coughing, the development of a pot belly and anaemia.

Heartworms are transmitted by mosquitoes. The mosquito drinks the blood of an infected dog and takes in larvae with the blood. The larvae, called microfilariae, develop within the body of the mosquito and are passed on to the next dog bitten after the larvae mature. It takes two to three weeks for the larvae to develop to the infective stage within the body of the mosquito. Dogs are usually treated at about six weeks of age and maintained on a prophylactic dose given monthly.

Blood testing for heartworms is not necessarily indicative of how seriously your dog is infected. Although this is a dangerous disease, it is not easy for a dog to be infected. Although heartworm is a major concern for dog owners in America, Australia, Asia and Central Europe, dog owners in the United Kingdom are just beginning to be concerned about heartworm. Discuss the various preventatives with your vet, as there are many different types now available. Together you can decide on a safe course of prevention for your dog.

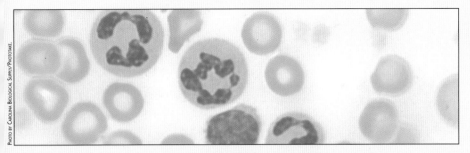

Magnified heart-worm larvae, *Dirofilaria immitis.*

PHOTO BY CAROLINA BIOLOGICAL SUPPLY/PHOTOTAKE.

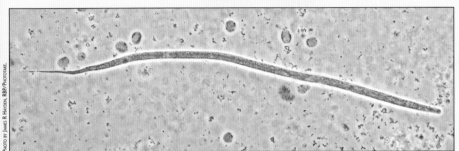

Heartworm, *Dirofilaria immitis.*

PHOTO BY JAMES R HAYDEN, RBP/PHOTOTAKE.

The heart of a dog infected with canine heart-worm, *Dirofilaria immitis.*

PHOTO BY JAMES R HAYDEN, RBP/PHOTOTAKE.

HOMEOPATHY:

an alternative
to conventional
medicine

'Less is Most'

Using this principle, the strength
of an homeopathic remedy is
measured by the number of
serial dilutions that were
undertaken to create it. The
greater the number of serial
dilutions, the greater the
strength of the homeopathic
remedy. The potency of a
remedy that has been made by
making a dilution of 1 part in
100 parts (or 1/100) is 1c or 1cH.
If this remedy is subjected to a
series of further dilutions, each
one being 1/100, a more dilute
and stronger remedy is
produced. If the remedy is
diluted in this way six times, it is
called 6c or 6cH. A dilution of 6c
is 1 part in 1,000,000,000,000. In
general, higher potencies in
more frequent doses are better
for acute symptoms and lower
potencies in more infrequent
doses are more useful for
chronic, long-standing problems.

**CURING OUR DOGS
NATURALLY**
Holistic medicine means treating
the whole animal as a unique,
perfect living being. Generally,
holistic treatments do not suppress
the symptoms that the body naturally produces, as do most medications prescribed by conventional
doctors and vets. Holistic methods
seek to cure disease by regaining
balance and harmony in the
patient's environment. Some of
these methods include use of nutritional therapy, herbs, flower
essences, aromatherapy, acupunc-
ture, massage, chiropractic and, of
course, the most popular holistic
approach, homeopathy.

Homeopathy is a theory or
system of treating illness with
small doses of substances which, if
administered in larger quantities,
would produce the symptoms that
the patient already has. This
approach is often described as 'like
cures like.' Although modern
veterinary medicine is geared
toward the 'quick fix,' homeopathy
relies on the belief that, given the
time, the body is able to heal itself
and return to its natural, healthy
state.

Choosing a remedy to cure a
problem in our dogs is the difficult
part of homeopathy. Consult with
your veterinary surgeon for a
professional diagnosis of your dog's
symptoms. Often these symptoms

require immediate conventional care. If your vet is willing and knowledgeable, you may attempt an homeopathic remedy. Be aware that cortisone prevents homeopathic remedies from working. There are hundreds of possibilities and combinations to cure many problems in dogs, from basic physical problems such as excessive moulting, fleas or other parasites, unattractive doggy odour, bad breath, upset tummy, obesity, dry,

oily or dull coat, diarrhoea, ear problems or eye discharge (including tears and dry or mucousy matter), to behavioural abnormalities such as fear of loud noises, habitual licking, poor appetite, excessive barking and various phobias. From alumina to zincum metallicum, the remedies span the planet and the imagination…from flowers and weeds to chemicals, insect droppings, diesel smoke and volcanic ash.

Using 'Like to Treat Like'

Unlike conventional medicines that suppress symptoms, homeopathic remedies treat illnesses with small doses of substances that, if administered in larger quantities, would produce the symptoms that the patient already has. While the same homeopathic remedy can be used to treat different symptoms in different dogs, here are some interesting remedies and their uses.

Apis Mellifica
(made from honey bee venom) can be used for allergies or to reduce swelling that occurs in acutely infected kidneys.

Diesel Smoke
can be used to help control travel sickness.

Calcarea Fluorica
(made from calcium fluoride, which helps harden bone structure) can be useful in treating hard lumps in tissues.

Natrum Muriaticum
(made from common salt, sodium chloride) is useful in treating thin, thirsty dogs.

Nitricum Acidum
(made from nitric acid) is used for symptoms you would expect to see from contact with acids, such as lesions, especially where the skin joins the linings of body orifices or openings such as the lips and nostrils.

Symphytum
(made from the herb Knitbone, *Symphytum officianale*) is used to encourage bones to heal.

Urtica Urens
(made from the common stinging nettle) is used in treating painful, irritating rashes.

Number-One Killer Disease in Dogs: CANCER

In every age, there is a word associated with a disease or plague that causes humans to shudder. In the 21st century, that word is 'cancer.' Just as cancer is the leading cause of death in humans, it claims nearly half the lives of dogs that die from a natural disease as well as half the dogs that die over the age of ten years.

Described as a genetic disease, cancer becomes a greater risk as the dog ages. Veterinary surgeons and dog owners have become increasingly aware of the threat of cancer to dogs. Statistics reveal that one dog in every five will develop cancer, the most common of which is skin cancer. Many cancers, including prostate, ovarian and breast cancer, can be avoided by spaying and neutering our dogs by the age of six months.

Early detection of cancer can save or extend your dog's life, so it is absolutely vital for owners to have their dogs examined by a qualified veterinary surgeon or oncologist immediately upon detection of any abnormality. Certain dietary guidelines have also proven to reduce the onset and spread of cancer. Foods based on fish rather than beef, due to the presence of Omega-3 fatty acids, are recommended. Other amino acids such as glutamine have significant benefits for canines, particularly those breeds that show a greater susceptibility to cancer.

Cancer management and treatments promise hope for future generations of canines. Since the disease is genetic, breeders should never breed a dog whose parents, grandparents and any related siblings have developed cancer. It is difficult to know whether to exclude an otherwise healthy dog from a breeding programme, as the disease does not manifest itself until the dog's senior years.

RECOGNISE CANCER WARNING SIGNS

Since early detection can possibly rescue your dog from becoming a cancer statistic, it is essential for owners to recognise the possible signs and seek the assistance of a qualified professional.

- Abnormal bumps or lumps that continue to grow
- Bleeding or discharge from any body cavity
- Persistent stiffness or lameness
- Recurrent sores or sores that do not heal
- Inappetence
- Breathing difficulties
- Weight loss
- Bad breath or odours
- General malaise and fatigue
- Eating and swallowing problems
- Difficulty urinating and defecating

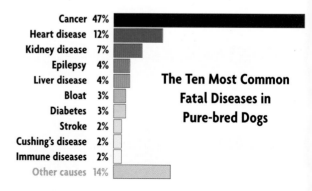

Disease	%
Cancer	47%
Heart disease	12%
Kidney disease	7%
Epilepsy	4%
Liver disease	4%
Bloat	3%
Diabetes	3%
Stroke	2%
Cushing's disease	2%
Immune diseases	2%
Other causes	14%

The Ten Most Common Fatal Diseases in Pure-bred Dogs

CDS: COGNITIVE DYSFUNCTION SYNDROME
'OLD-DOG SYNDROME'

There are many ways to evaluate old-dog syndrome. Veterinary surgeons have defined CDS (cognitive dysfunction syndrome) as the gradual deterioration of cognitive abilities. These are indicated by changes in the dog's behaviour. When a dog changes its routine response, and maladies have been eliminated as the cause of these behavioural changes, then CDS is the usual diagnosis.

More than half the dogs over eight years old suffer from some form of CDS. The older the dog, the more chance it has of suffering from CDS. In humans, doctors often dismiss the CDS behavioural changes as part of 'winding down.'

There are four major signs of CDS: the dog has frequent toilet accidents inside the home, sleeps much more or much less than normal, acts confused and fails to respond to social stimuli.

SYMPTOMS OF CDS

FREQUENT TOILET ACCIDENTS
- Urinates in the house.
- Defecates in the house.
- Doesn't signal that he wants to go out.

SLEEP PATTERNS
- Awakens more slowly.
- Sleeps more than normal during the day.
- Sleeps less during the night.

CONFUSION
- Goes outside and just stands there.
- Appears confused with a faraway look in his eyes.
- Hides more often.
- Doesn't recognise friends.
- Doesn't come when called.
- Walks around listlessly and without a destination.

FAILS TO RESPOND TO SOCIAL STIMULI
- Comes to people less frequently, whether called or not.
- Doesn't tolerate petting for more than a short time.
- Doesn't come to the door when you return home.

MANCHESTER TERRIER

The term *old* is a qualitative term. For dogs, as well as their masters, old is relative. Certainly we can all distinguish between a puppy Manchester and an adult Manchester—there are the obvious physical traits, such as size, appearance and facial expressions, and personality traits. Puppies and young dogs like to play with children. Children's natural exuberance is a good match for the seemingly endless energy of young dogs. They like to run, jump, chase and retrieve. When dogs grow older and cease their interaction with children, they are often thought of as being too old to play with the children.

On the other hand, if a Manchester is only exposed to people who live quieter lifestyles, his life will normally be less active and the decrease in his activity level as he gets older will not be as obvious.

If people live to be 100 years old, dogs live to be 20 years old. While this may sound like a good rule of thumb, it is very inaccurate. When trying to compare dog years to human years, you cannot make a generalisation about all dogs. Terriers as a whole are long-lived dogs and your Manchester Terrier will be no different. If your dog lives to 8 years of age, he will likely live until 12 years of age

GETTING OLD
The bottom line is simply that your dog is getting old when *you* think he is getting old because he slows down in his level of general activity, including walking, running, eating, jumping and retrieving. On the other hand, the frequency of certain activities increases, such as more sleeping, more barking and more repetition of habits like going to the door without being called when you put your coat on to leave the house.

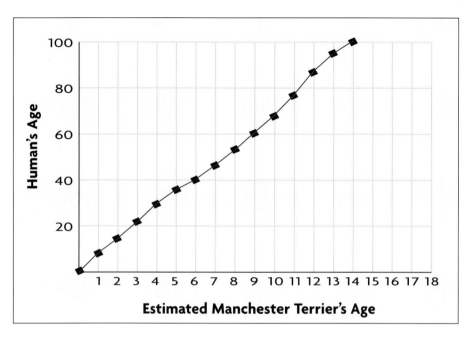

Estimated Manchester Terrier's Age

and, for a Manchester, it is not unusual for him to live to 15 years of age. Take care of your pet, feed him well, take him to a vet for his routine visits and for any problems and keep him on a lead or in a fenced garden, and chances are your dog will be with you for a long life.

Dogs are generally considered mature within three years, but they can reproduce even earlier. So the first three years of a dog's life are like seven times that of comparable humans. That means a 3-year-old dog is like a 21-year-old human. As the curve of comparison shows, there is no hard and fast rule for comparing dog and human ages. The comparison is made even more difficult, for not all humans age at the same rate...and human females live longer than human males.

WHAT TO LOOK FOR IN VETERANS

Most veterinary surgeons and behaviourists use the seven-year mark as the time to consider a dog a veteran. The term *veteran* does not imply that the dog is geriatric and has begun to fail in mind and body. Ageing is essentially a slowing process. Humans readily admit that they feel a difference in their activity level from age 20 to 30, and then from 30 to 40, etc. By treating the seven-year-old dog as a veteran, owners are able to implement certain therapeutic and preventative medical strategies with the help of their veterinary surgeons. A special-care programme should include at least two veterinary visits per year and screening sessions to determine the dog's health status, as well as nutritional counselling. Veterinary surgeons determine the veteran dog's health status through a blood smear for a complete blood count, serum chemistry profile with electrolytes, urinalysis, blood pressure check, electrocardiogram, ocular tonometry (pressure on the eyeball) and dental prophylaxis.

Such an extensive programme for veteran dogs is well advised before owners start to see the obvious physical signs of ageing, such as slower and inhibited movement, greying, increased sleep/nap periods and disinterest in play and other activity. This preventative programme promises a longer, healthier life for the ageing dog. Among the physical problems common in ageing dogs are the loss of sight and hearing, arthritis, kidney and liver failure, diabetes mellitus, heart disease and Cushing's disease (an hormonal disease).

In addition to the physical manifestations discussed, there are some behavioural changes and problems related to ageing dogs. Dogs suffering from hearing or vision loss, dental discomfort or arthritis can become aggressive. Likewise, the near-deaf and/or blind dog may be startled more easily and react in an unexpectedly aggressive manner. Veterans suffering from senility can become more impatient and irritable. Housesoiling accidents are associated with loss of mobility, kidney problems and loss of sphincter

NOTICING THE SYMPTOMS

The symptoms listed below are symptoms that gradually appear and become more noticeable. They are not life-threatening; however, the symptoms below are to be taken very seriously and warrant a discussion with your veterinary surgeon:

• Your dog cries and whimpers when he moves, and he stops running completely.

• Convulsions start or become more serious and frequent. The usual convulsion (spasm) is when the dog stiffens and starts to tremble, being unable or unwilling to move. The seizure usually lasts for 5 to 30 minutes.

• Your dog drinks more water and urinates more frequently. Wetting and bowel accidents take place indoors without warning.

• Vomiting becomes more and more frequent.

control as well as plaque accumulation, physiological brain changes and reactions to medications. Older dogs, just like young puppies, suffer from separation anxiety, which can lead to excessive barking, whining, housesoiling and destructive behaviour. Veterans may become fearful of everyday sounds, such as vacuum cleaners, heaters, thunder and passing traffic. Some dogs have difficulty sleeping, due to discomfort, the need for frequent toilet visits and the like.

Owners should avoid spoiling the older dog with too many treats. Obesity is a common problem in older dogs and subtracts years from their lives. Keep the veteran dog as trim as possible, since excess weight puts additional stress on the body's vital organs. Some breeders recommend supplementing the diet with foods high in fibre and lower in calories. Adding fresh vegetables and marrow broth to the veteran's diet makes a tasty, low-calorie, low-fat supplement. Vets also offer speciality diets for veteran dogs that are worth exploring.

Your dog, as he nears his twilight years, needs your patience and good care more than ever. Never punish an older dog for an accident or abnormal behaviour. For all the years of love, protection and companionship that your dog has provided,

AGEING SIGNS

An old dog starts to show one or more of the following symptoms:

• The hair on the face and paws starts to turn grey. The colour breakdown usually starts around the eyes and mouth.

• Sleep patterns are deeper and longer, and the old dog is harder to awaken.

• Food intake diminishes.

• Responses to calls, whistles and other signals are ignored more and more.

• Eye contact does not evoke tail wagging (assuming it once did).

he deserves special attention and courtesies. The older dog may need to relieve himself at 3 a.m. because he can no longer hold it

Your Manchester does not understand why his world is slowing down. Owners must make their dogs' transition into the golden years as pleasant and rewarding as possible.

WHAT TO DO WHEN THE TIME COMES

You are never fully prepared to make a rational decision about putting your dog to sleep. It is very obvious that you love your Manchester or you would not be reading this book. Putting a loved dog to sleep is extremely difficult. It is a decision that must be made with your veterinary surgeon. You are usually forced to make the decision when your dog experiences one or more life-threatening symptoms, requiring you to seek veterinary help.

For the many years of devotion your Manchester Terrier has provided you, special care during his veteran years is a small price to pay.

for eight hours. Older dogs may not be able to remain crated for more than two or three hours. It may be time to give up a sofa or chair to your old friend. Although he may not seem as enthusiastic about your attention and petting, he does appreciate the considerations you offer as he gets older.

TO THE RESCUE

Some people choose to adopt or 'rescue' an older dog instead of buying a new puppy. Some older dogs may have come from abusive environments and be fearful, while other dogs may have developed many bad habits; both situations can present challenges to their new owners. Training an older dog will take more time and patience, but persistence and an abundance of praise and love can transform a dog into a well-behaved, loyal companion.

If the prognosis of the malady indicates the end is near and your beloved pet will only suffer more and experience no enjoyment for the balance of his life, then euthanasia is the right choice.

WHAT IS EUTHANASIA?
Euthanasia derives from the Greek, meaning *good death*. In other words, it means the planned, painless killing of a dog suffering from a painful, incurable condition, or who is so aged that he cannot walk, see, eat or control his excretory functions.

Euthanasia is usually accomplished by injection with an overdose of an anaesthesia or barbiturate. Aside from the prick of the needle, the experience is usually painless.

MAKING THE DECISION
The decision to euthanise your dog is never easy. The days during which the dog becomes ill and the end occurs can be unusually stressful for you. If this is your first experience with the death of a loved one, you may need the comfort dictated by your religious beliefs. If you are the head of the family and have children, you should have involved them in the decision of putting your Manchester to sleep. Usually your dog can be maintained on drugs at the vet's for a

---

EUTHANASIA SERVICES
Euthanasia must be performed by a licenced veterinary surgeon. There also may be societies for the prevention of cruelty to animals in your area. They often offer this service upon a vet's recommendation.

---

few days in order to give you ample time to make a decision. During this time, talking with members of your family or people who have lived through this experience can ease the burden of your inevitable decision.

THE FINAL RESTING PLACE
Dogs can have some of the same privileges as humans. The remains of your beloved dog can be buried in a pet cemetery, which is generally expensive. Alternatively, dogs can be cremated individually and the ashes returned to their owners. A less expensive option is mass cremation, although, of course, the ashes of individual dogs cannot then be returned. Vets can usually arrange these services on your behalf. The cost of these options should always be discussed frankly and openly with your veterinary surgeon. In Britain, if your dog has died at the surgery, the vet legally cannot allow you to take your dog's body home because home burials are unlawful.

GETTING ANOTHER DOG

The grief of losing your beloved dog will be as lasting as the grief of losing a human friend or relative. In most cases, if your dog died of old age (if there is such a thing), he had slowed down considerably. Do you want a new Manchester puppy to replace him? Or are you better off finding a more mature Manchester, say two to three years of age, which will usually be house-trained and will have an already developed personality. In this case, you can find out if you like each other after a few hours of being together.

The decision is, of course, your own. Do you want another Manchester or perhaps a different breed so as to avoid comparison with your beloved friend? Most people usually stay with the same breed because they know and love the traits of that breed. Then, too, they often know people who have the same breed and perhaps they are lucky enough that a breeder they know expects a litter soon. What could be better?

COPING WITH LOSS

When your dog dies, you may be as upset as when a human companion passes away. You are losing your protector, your baby, your confidante and your best friend. Many people experience not only grief but also feelings of guilt and doubt as to whether they did all that they could for their pet. Allow yourself to grieve and mourn, and seek help from friends and support groups. You may also wish to consult books and websites that deal with this topic.

Your vet can help you locate a pet cemetery in your vicinity if you choose this way of memorialising your dog.

When you purchased your Manchester Terrier, you should have made it clear to the breeder whether you wanted one just as a loveable companion and pet, or if you hoped to be buying a Manchester Terrier with show prospects. No reputable breeder will have sold you a young puppy saying that it was *definitely* of show quality, for so much can go wrong during the early months of a puppy's development. If you plan to show, what you hopefully have acquired is a puppy with 'show potential.'

To the novice, exhibiting a Manchester Terrier in the show ring may look easy, but it takes a lot of hard work and devotion to do top winning at a show such as the prestigious Crufts Dog Show, not to mention a little luck too!

The first concept that the canine novice learns when watching a dog show is that each dog first competes against members of his own breed. Once the judge has selected the best member of each breed, provided that the show is judged on a Group system, that chosen dog will compete with other dogs in his group. Finally, each Group winner will compete for Best in Show.

The second concept that you must understand is that the dogs are not actually competing against one another. The judge compares each dog against the breed standard, which is a written description of the ideal specimen of the breed. While some early breed standards were indeed based on specific dogs that were famous or popular, many dedi-

The winning Manchester Terrier is the dog whom the judge determines is closest to the ideal dog described in the breed standard.

cated enthusiasts say that a perfect specimen, as described in the standard, has never walked into a show ring, has never been bred and, to the woe of dog breeders around the globe, does not exist. Breeders attempt to get as close to this ideal as possible with every litter, but theoretically the

'perfect' dog is so elusive that it is impossible to breed.

If you are interested in exploring dog shows, your best bet is to join your local breed club. These clubs often host both Championship and Open Shows, and sometimes Match meetings and special events, all of which could be of interest, even if you are only an onlooker. Clubs also send out newsletters and some organise training days and seminars in order that people may learn more about their chosen breed. To locate the breed club closest to you, contact The Kennel Club, the ruling body for the British dog world. The Kennel Club governs not only conformation shows but also working trials, obedience shows and agility trials. The Kennel Club furnishes the rules and regulations for all these events plus general dog registration and other basic requirements of dog ownership. Its annual show, called the Crufts Dog Show, held in Birmingham, is the largest benched show in England. Every year over 20,000 of the UK's best dogs qualify to participate in this marvellous show, which lasts four days.

The Kennel Club governs many different kinds of shows in Great Britain, Australia, South Africa and beyond. At the most competitive and prestigious of these shows, the Championship Shows, a dog can earn Challenge

NATIONAL MANCHESTER TERRIER CLUBS

As the breed continues to gain new followers around the world, the national or parent club helps to disperse much-needed accurate information. In the UK, contact the British Manchester Terrier Club; in the US, the American Manchester Terrier Club; in Canada, the Canadian Manchester Terrier Club; in Australia, the Manchester Terrier Club of New South Wales, Australia; and in Finland, the Finnish Manchester Terrier Club.

Certificates, and thereby become a Show Champion or a Champion. A dog must earn three Challenge Certificates (CCs) under three different judges to earn the prefix of 'Sh Ch' or 'Ch.' Note that some breeds must also qualify in a field trial in order to gain the title of full Champion, though the Manchester is not such a breed. CCs are awarded to a very small percentage of the dogs competing, and dogs that are already Champions compete with others for these coveted CCs. The number of Challenge Certificates awarded in any one year is based upon the total number of dogs in

INFORMATION ON CLUBS

You can get information about dog shows from kennel clubs and breed clubs:

The Kennel Club
1-5 Clarges St., Piccadilly, London W1Y 8AB
UK
www.the-kennel-club.org.uk

Fédération Cynologique Internationale
14, rue Leopold II, B-6530 Thuin, Belgium
www.fci.be

American Kennel Club
5580 Centerview Dr., Raleigh, NC 27606-3390
USA
www.akc.org

Canadian Kennel Club
89 Skyway Ave., Suite 100, Etobicoke,
Ontario
M9W 6R4 Canada
www.ckc.ca

each breed entered for competition. There are three types of Championship Shows: an all-breed General Championship Show, for all Kennel-Club-recognised breeds; a Group Championship Show, which is limited to breeds within one of the groups; and a Breed Show, which is usually confined to a single breed. The Kennel Club determines which breeds at which Championship Shows will have the opportunity to earn CCs (or tickets). Serious exhibitors often will opt not to participate if the tickets are withheld at a particular show. This makes earning championships even more difficult to accomplish.

Open Shows are generally less competitive and are frequently used as 'practice shows' for young dogs. There are hundreds of Open

The dog that wins his class continues on for Best of Breed and, in a Group show, then competes for Best in Group and finally Best in Show.

Shows each year that can be delightful social events and are great first show experiences for the novice. Even if you're considering just watching a show to wet your paws, an Open Show is a great choice.

While Championship and Open Shows are most important for the beginner to understand, there are other types of shows in which the interested dog owner can participate. Training clubs sponsor Matches that can be entered on the day of the show for a nominal fee. In these introductory-level exhibitions, two dogs' names are pulled out of a hat and 'matched,' the winner of that match goes on to the next round and eventually only one dog is left undefeated.

Exemption Shows are much more light-hearted affairs with usually only four pedigree classes and several 'fun' classes, all of which can be entered on the day of the show. Exemption Shows are sometimes held in conjunction with small agricultural shows and the proceeds must be given to a charity. Limited Shows are also available in small number, but entry is restricted to members of the club that hosts the show, although one can usually join the club when making an entry.

Before you actually step into the ring, you would be well advised to sit back and observe the judge's ring procedure. If it is your

> **MANCHESTERS ON THE WEB**
> Both the British Manchester Terrier Club and the American Manchester Terrier Club have excellent websites and the prospective buyer of a Manchester Terrier should look over their information on the breed. Visit www.manchester-terrier-club.org.uk for the British club and www.clubs.akc.org/mtca.

first time in the ring, do not be over-anxious and run to the front of the line. It is much better to stand back and study how the exhibitor in front of you is performing. The judge asks each handler to 'stand' the dog, hopefully showing the dog off to his best advantage. The judge will observe the dog from a distance and from different angles, approach the dog, check his teeth, overall structure, alertness and muscle tone, as well as consider how well the dog 'conforms' to the standard. Most importantly, the judge will have the exhibitor move the dog around the ring in some pattern that he should specify (another advantage to not going first, but always listen since some judges change their directions, and the judge is always right!). Finally the judge will give the dog one last look before moving on to the next exhibitor.

If you are not in the top three

at your first show, do not be discouraged. Be patient and consistent, and you may eventually find yourself in the winning line-up. Remember that the winners were once in your shoes and have devoted many hours and much money to earn the placement. If you find that your dog is losing every time and never getting a nod, it may be time to consider a different dog sport or just enjoy your Manchester Terrier as a pet.

WORKING TRIALS
Working trials can be entered by any well-trained dog of any breed, not just Gundogs or Working dogs. Many dogs that earn the Kennel Club Good Citizen Dog award choose to participate in a working trial. There are five stakes at both open and championship levels: Companion Dog (CD), Utility Dog (UD), Working Dog (WD), Tracking Dog (TD) and Patrol Dog (PD). As in conformation shows, dogs compete against a standard; if the dog reaches the qualifying mark, he obtains a certificate. Divided into groups, each exercise must be achieved 70% in order for the dog to qualify. If the dog achieves 80% in the open level, he receives a Certificate of Merit (COM); in the championship level, he receives a Qualifying Certificate. At the CD stake, dogs must participate in four groups: Control, Stay, Agility and Search (Retrieve and Nosework). At the next three levels, UD, WD

and TD, there are only three groups: Control, Agility and Nosework.

Agility consists of three jumps: a vertical scale up a 2-metre wall of planks; a clear jump over a basic 1-metre hurdle with a removable top bar; and a long jump across angled planks stretching 3 metres.

To earn the UD, WD and TD, dogs must track approximately one-half mile for articles laid from one-half hour to three hours previously. Tracks consist of turns and legs, and fresh ground is used for each participant. The fifth stake, PD, involves teaching manwork, which is not recommended for every breed.

AGILITY TRIALS
Agility trials began in the UK in 1977 and have since spread

Natural show dogs, sleek, obedient and handsome, Manchesters make brilliant participants at dog shows.

around the world, and Manchesters can do brilliantly in this exciting sport. The handler directs his dog over an obstacle course that includes jumps (such as those used in the working trials), as well as tyres, the dog walk, weave poles, pipe tunnels, collapsed tunnels, etc. The Kennel Club requires that dogs not be trained for agility until they are 12 months old. This dog sport is great fun for dog and

The picture of versatility and agility, the Manchester knows no bounds.

owner, and interested owners should join a training club that has obstacles and experienced agility handlers who can introduce you and your dog to the 'ropes' (and tyres, tunnels, etc.).

FÉDÉRATION CYNOLOGIQUE INTERNATIONALE
Established in 1911, the Fédération Cynologique Internationale (FCI) represents the 'world kennel club.' This international body brings uniformity to the breeding, judging and showing of pure-bred dogs. Although the FCI originally included only five European nations: France, Germany, Austria, the Netherlands and Belgium (which remains its headquarters), the organisation today embraces nations on six continents and recognises well over 300 breeds of pure-bred dog.

There are three titles attainable through the FCI: the International Champion, which is the most prestigious; the International Beauty Champion, which is based on aptitude certificates in different countries; and the International Trial Champion, which is based on achievement in obedience trials in different countries. The FCI sponsors both national and international shows. The hosting country determines the judging system and breed standards are always based on the breed's country of origin. Dogs

Manchesters excel at agility trials and have qualified to compete in top events.

from every country can partici-pate in these impressive canine spectacles, the largest of which is the World Dog Show, hosted in a different country each year.

The FCI is divided into ten 'Groups' and the Manchester Terrier competes in Group 3 (for Terriers). At an all-breed FCI show, the following classes are offered for each breed: Puppy Class (6–9 months), Junior Class (9–18 months), Open Class (15 months or older) and Champion Class. A dog can be awarded a classification of Excellent, Very Good, Good, Sufficient and Not Sufficient. Puppies can be awarded classifications of Very Promising, Promising or Not Promising. Four placements are made in each class. After all classes are judged, a Best of Breed is selected. Other special groups and classes may also be shown. Each exhibitor showing a dog receives a written evaluation from the judge.

Besides the World Dog Show and European Champions Show, you can exhibit your dog at speciality shows held by different breed clubs. Speciality shows may have their own regulations.

As a Manchester Terrier owner, you have selected your dog so that you and your loved ones can have a companion, a protector, a friend and a four-legged family member. You invest time, money and effort to care for and train the family's new charge. Of course, this chosen canine behaves perfectly! Well, perfectly *like a dog.*

THINK LIKE A DOG

Dogs do not think like humans, nor do humans think like dogs, though we try. Unfortunately, a dog is incapable of comprehending how humans think, so the responsibility falls on the owner to adopt a viable canine mindset. Many a dog owner makes the mistake in training of thinking that he can reprimand his dog for something the dog did a while ago. Manchesters, by one year of age, learn right from wrong and develop 'consciences.' While an owner cannot chastise a Manchester Terrier for a misdeed an hour later, you can correct him soon after.

The following behavioural problems represent some which owners most commonly encounter. Every dog is unique and every situation is unique. No author could purport for you to solve your Manchester Terrier's problems simply by reading a chapter. Here we outline some basic 'dogspeak' so that owners' chances of solving behavioural problems are increased. Discuss bad habits with your breeder first, then you can contact your veterinary surgeon and perhaps he can recommend a behavioural specialist to consult in appropriate cases. Since behavioural abnormalities are the main reason that owners abandon their pets, we hope that you will make a valiant effort to solve your Manchester Terrier's problems. Patience and understanding are virtues that must dwell in every pet-loving household.

AGGRESSION

This is a problem that concerns all responsible dog owners, and terrier owners understand that their dogs are naturally aggressive, to a degree. Aggression, when not controlled always becomes

Learn to read your dog's body language: these two chaps are pleased to see one another.

dangerous. An aggressive dog, no matter the size, may lunge at, bite or even attack a person or another dog. Aggressive behaviour is not to be tolerated. It is more than just inappropriate behaviour; it is painful for a family to watch their dog become unpredictable in his behaviour to the point where they are afraid of him. While not all aggressive behaviour is dangerous, growling, baring teeth, etc., can be frightening. It is important to ascertain why the dog is acting in this manner. Aggression is a display of dominance, and the dog should not have the dominant role in his pack, which is, in this case, your family.

It is important not to challenge an aggressive dog, as this could provoke an attack. Observe your Manchester Terrier's body language. Does he make direct eye contact and stare? Does he try to make himself as large as possible: ears pricked, chest out, tail erect? Height and size signify authority in a dog pack—being taller or 'above' another dog literally means that he is 'above' in social status. These body signals tell you that your Manchester Terrier thinks he is in charge, a problem that needs to be addressed. An aggressive dog is unpredictable; you never know when he is going to strike and what he is going to do. You cannot understand why a dog that is playful one minute is growling the next.

Fear is a common cause of aggression in dogs. If you can isolate what brings out the fear reaction, you can help the dog overcome it. Supervise your Manchester Terrier's interactions with people and other dogs, and praise the dog when it goes well. If he starts to act aggressively in a situation, correct him and remove him from the situation. Do not let people approach the dog and start petting him without your express permission. That way, you can have the dog sit to accept petting, and praise him when he behaves properly. You are focusing on praise and on modifying his behaviour by rewarding him when he acts appropriately. By being gentle and by supervising his interactions, you are showing him that there is no need to be afraid or defensive.

The best solution is to consult your breeder, since he should have the most experience with the Manchester. Together, perhaps

Manchesters are not as aggressive as most other terriers. They are playful dogs that enjoy a friendly game of roughhouse with a black and tan chum.

NO EYE CONTACT
DANGER! If you and your on-lead dog are approached by a larger, running dog that is not restrained, walk away from the dog as quickly as possible. Do not allow your dog to make eye contact with the other dog. You should not make eye contact either. In dog terms, eye contact indicates a challenge.

you can pinpoint the cause of your dog's aggression and do something about it. An aggressive dog cannot be trusted, and a dog that cannot be trusted is not safe to have as a family pet. If, very unusually, you find that your pet has become untrustworthy and you feel it necessary to seek a new home with a more suitable family and environment, explain fully to the new owners all your reasons for rehoming the dog to be fair to all concerned. In the *very worst* case, you will have to consider euthanasia.

AGGRESSION TOWARD OTHER DOGS
A dog's aggressive behaviour toward another dog sometimes stems from insufficient exposure to other dogs at an early age, though terriers (especially males) are not bred to 'like other dogs.' If other dogs make your Manchester Terrier nervous and agitated, he will lash out as a defensive mechanism, though this behaviour is

When two dogs meet, they engage in an age-old canine ritual of sniffing and posturing. Dog fights are usually instigated by nervous owners tugging at their dogs' leads.

thankfully uncommon in the breed. A dog who has not received sufficient exposure to other canines tends to believe that he is the only dog on the planet. The animal becomes so dominant that he does not even show signs that he is fearful or threatened. Without growling or any other physical signal as a warning, he will lunge at and bite the other dog. A way to correct this is to let your Manchester Terrier approach another dog when walking on lead. Watch very closely and at the very first sign of aggression, correct your Manchester Terrier and pull him away. Scold him for any sign of discomfort, and then praise him when he ignores or tolerates the other dog. Keep this up until he stops the aggressive behaviour, learns to ignore the other dog or accepts other dogs. Praise him lavishly for his correct behaviour.

PUPPY THREATS

Never allow your puppy to growl at you or bare his tiny teeth. Such behaviour is dominant and aggressive. If not corrected, the dog will repeat the behaviour, which will become more threatening as he grows larger and will eventually lead to biting.

DOMINANT AGGRESSION

A social hierarchy is firmly established in a wild dog pack. The dog wants to dominate those under him and please those above him. Dogs know that there must

PHARMACEUTICAL FIX

There are two drugs specifically designed to treat mental problems in dogs. About 7 million dogs each year are destroyed because owners can no longer tolerate their dogs' behaviour, according to Nicholas Dodman, a specialist in animal behaviour at Tufts University in Massachusetts.

The first drug, Clomicalm, is prescribed for dogs suffering from separation anxiety, which is said to cause them to react when left alone by barking, chewing their owners' belongings, drooling copiously or defecating or urinating inside the home.

The second drug, Anipryl, is recommended for cognitive dysfunction syndrome or 'old-dog syndrome,' a mental deterioration that comes with age. Such dogs often seem to forget that they were house-trained and where their food bowls are, and they may even fail to recognise their owners.

A tremendous human-animal bonding relationship is established with all dogs, particularly veteran dogs. This precious relationship deteriorates when the dog does not recognise his master. The drug can restore the bond and make veteran dogs feel more like their old selves.

be a leader. If you are not the obvious choice for emperor, the dog will assume the throne! These conflicting innate desires are what a dog owner confronts when he sets about training a dog. In training a dog to obey commands, the owner is reinforcing that he is the top dog in the pack and that the dog should, and should want to, serve his superior. Thus, the owner is suppressing the dog's urge to dominate by modifying his behaviour and making him obedient.

An important part of training is taking every opportunity to reinforce that you are the leader. The simple action of making your Manchester Terrier sit to wait for his food says that you control

when he eats and that he is dependent on you for food. Although it may be difficult, do not give in to your dog's wishes every time he whines or looks at you with his pleading eyes. It is a constant effort to show the dog that his place in the pack is at the bottom. This is not meant to sound cruel or inhumane. You love your Manchester Terrier and you should treat him with care and affection. You likely did not get a dog just so you could boss about another creature. Dog training is not about being cruel, it is about moulding the dog's behaviour into what is acceptable and teaching him to live by your rules. In theory, it is quite simple: catch him in appropriate behaviour and reward him for it. Add a dog into the equation and it becomes a bit more trying, but as a rule of thumb, positive reinforcement is what works best.

With a dominant dog, punishment and negative reinforcement can have the opposite effect from what you desire. It can make a dog fearful and/or act out aggressively if he feels he is being challenged. Remember, a dominant dog perceives himself at the top of the social heap and will fight to defend his perceived status. The best way to prevent that is never to give him reason to think that he is in control in the first place. If you are having trouble training your Manchester Terrier and it seems as if he is constantly challenging your authority, seek the

help of an obedience trainer or behavioural specialist. A professional will work with both you and your dog to teach you effective techniques to use at home. Beware of trainers who rely on excessively harsh methods; scolding is necessary now and then, but the focus in your training should always be on positive reinforcement.

DIGGING

Digging, which is seen as a destructive behaviour to humans, is actually quite a natural behaviour in dogs, especially for the terriers who were 'born to dig.' The Manchester, however, is not a digger like his terrier brethren, as the breed was designed to hunt and run, not to dig. When digging occurs in your garden, it is actually a normal behaviour redirected into something the dog can do in his everyday life. Most terriers will dig at the slightest whiff of passing rat or mouse. In the wild, a dog would be actively seeking food, making his own shelter, etc. He would be using his paws in a purposeful manner for his survival. Since you provide him with food and shelter, he has no need to use his paws for these purposes, and so the energy that he would be using may manifest itself in the form of little holes all over your garden and flower beds.

Perhaps your dog is digging as a reaction to boredom—it is some-

---

FEAR IN A GROWN DOG

Fear in a grown dog is often the result of improper or incomplete socialisation as a pup, or it can be the result of a traumatic experience he suffered when young. Keep in mind that the term 'traumatic' is relative—something that you would not think twice about can leave a lasting negative impression on a puppy. If the dog experiences a similar experience later in life, he may try to fight back to protect himself. Again, this behaviour is very unpredictable, especially if you do not know what is triggering his fear.

Digging is a normal canine pastime. The very name 'terrier' derives from the Latin base word *terra*, meaning earth. Manchester Terriers are not digging terriers, *per se*, but they are also not afraid to get their paws dirty!

what similar to someone eating a whole bag of crisps in front of the TV—because they are there and there is nothing better to do! Basically, the answer is to provide the dog with adequate play and exercise so that his mind and paws are occupied, and so that he feels as if he is doing something useful.

Of course, digging is easiest to control if it is stopped as soon as possible, but it is often hard to catch a dog in the act. If your dog is a compulsive digger and is not easily distracted by other activities, you can designate an area on your property where he is allowed

to dig. If you catch him digging in an off-limits area of the garden, immediately bring him to the approved area and praise him for digging there. Keep a close eye on him so that you can catch him in the act—that is the best way to make him understand what is permitted and what is not.

SEXUAL BEHAVIOUR
Dogs exhibit certain sexual behaviours that may have influenced your choice of male or female when you first purchased your Manchester Terrier. To a certain extent, spaying/neutering will eliminate these behaviours,

but if you are purchasing a dog that you wish to breed from, you should be aware of what you will have to deal with throughout the dog's life.

Female dogs usually have two oestruses per year, with each season lasting about three weeks. These are the only times in which a female dog will mate, and she usually will not allow this until the second week of the cycle, but this does vary from bitch to bitch. If not bred during the heat cycle, it is not uncommon for a bitch to experience a false pregnancy, in which her mammary glands swell and she exhibits maternal tendencies toward toys or other objects.

Male dogs tend to be wanderers, especially when not neutered, always looking for a bitch in season. Along the same line, male dogs will mark their perceived territory with small amounts of their potent urine. A male believes that your entire house and garden are 'his' territory, and he will have no reservations lifting his mighty leg on your draperies or sofa. Males, mistakenly thinking that they are the stronger sex, also can develop the habit of mounting objects (your leg or a good-smelling friend's leg, usually) to prove how 'macho' they are. Your male may attach on to your leg with considerable strength, as mounting is not a game but an effort to 'save the race.' Owners must recognise that mounting is not only a sexual expression but also one of dominance, seen in males and females alike. Be consistent and persistent and you will find that you can 'move mounters.'

MACHO GUSTO

Males, whether castrated or not, will mount almost anything: a pillow, your leg or, much to your horror, even your neighbour's leg. As with other types of inappropriate behaviour, the dog must be corrected while in the act, which for once is not difficult. Often he will not let go! While a puppy is experimenting with his very first urges, his owners feel he needs to 'sow his oats' and allow the pup to mount. As the pup grows into a full-size dog, with full-size urges, it becomes a nuisance and an embarrassment. Males always appear as if they are trying to 'save the race,' more determined and stronger than imaginable. While altering the dog at an appropriate age will limit the dog's desire, it usually does not remove it entirely.

CHEWING

The international canine pastime is chewing! Every dog loves to sink his 'canines' into a tasty bone, or whatever is available! Dogs need to chew, to massage their gums, to make their new teeth feel better and to exercise their jaws. This is a natural behaviour deeply embedded in all things canine. Your role as owner is not to stop the dog's chewing, but to redirect it to positive, chew-worthy objects. Be an informed owner and purchase

NO JUMPING

Stop a dog from jumping up before he jumps. If he is getting ready to jump onto you, simply walk away. If he jumps up on you before you can turn away, lift your knee so that it bumps him in the chest. Do not be forceful. Your dog soon will realise that jumping up is not a productive way of getting attention.

proper chew toys like strong nylon bones that will not splinter. Be sure that the objects are safe and durable, since your dog's safety is at risk. Again, the owner is responsible for ensuring a dog-proof environment. The best answer is prevention, that is, put your shoes, handbags and other tasty objects in their proper places (out of the reach of the growing canine mouth). Direct your puppy to his toys whenever you see him tasting the furniture legs or the leg of your trousers. Make a loud noise to attract the pup's attention, immediately escort him to his chew toy and engage him with the toy for at least four minutes, praising and encouraging him all the while.

Some trainers recommend deterrents, such as hot pepper, a bitter spice or a product designed for this purpose, to discourage the dog from chewing unwanted objects. Test these products with your dog before investing in large quantities.

JUMPING UP

Jumping up is a dog's friendly way of saying hello! Some dog owners do not mind when their dog jumps up. The problem arises when guests come to the house and the dog greets them in the same manner—whether they like it or not! However friendly the greeting may be, the chances are that your visitors will not appreci-

Don't encourage jumping games with your Manchester Terrier. Once bad habits are formed, they are very difficult to eradicate.

ate your dog's enthusiasm. The dog will not be able to distinguish upon whom he can jump and whom he cannot. Therefore, it is probably best to discourage this

DOG TALK

Deciphering your dog's barks is very similar to understanding a baby's cries: there is a different cry for eating, sleeping, toilet needs, etc. Your dog talks to you not only through howls and groans but also through his body language. Baring teeth, staring and inflating the chest are all threatening gestures. If a dog greets you by licking his nose, turning his head or yawning, these are friendly, peacemaking gestures.

behaviour entirely.

Pick a command such as 'Off' (avoid using 'Down' since you will use that for the dog to lie down) and tell him 'Off' when he jumps up. Place him on the ground on all fours and have him sit, praising him the whole time. Always lavish him with praise and petting when he is in the sit position. In this way you can give him a warm affectionate greeting, let him know that you are as pleased to see him as he is to see you and instil good manners at the same time!

BARKING

Manchesters are blest with loud, clear barks, which they use to protect their territories. These are competent, reliable watchdogs, and a good bark is a watchdog's first line of defence. Unlike smaller short-legged terriers, the Manchester is not a yappy dog. He barks for good reason, though it is important to teach your dog what's a valid cause for alarm and what is not. Some dogs, impressed by the sound of their own mellifluous voices, will bark at every falling leaf or passing car.

How purposeful is your Manchester's bark? That needs to be determined. If an intruder attempted to break into your home in the middle of the night and your Manchester Terrier barked a warning, wouldn't you be pleased? You would probably

HE'S PROTECTING YOU

Barking is your dog's way of protecting you. If he barks at a stranger walking past your house, a moving car or a fleeing cat, he is merely exercising his responsibility to protect his pack *(you)* and territory from a perceived intruder. Since the 'intruder' usually keeps going, the dog thinks his barking chased it away and he feels fulfilled. This behaviour leads your overly vocal friend to believe that he is the 'dog in charge.'

deem your dog a hero, a wonderful guardian and protector of the home. On the other hand, if a friend drops by unexpectedly and rings the doorbell and is greeted with a sudden sharp bark, you would probably be annoyed at the dog. But in reality, isn't this just the same behaviour? The dog does not know any better...unless he sees who is at the door and it is someone he knows, he will bark as a means of vocalising that his (and your) territory is being threatened. While your friend is not posing a threat, it is all the same to the dog. Barking is his means of letting you know that there is an intrusion, whether friend or foe, on your property. This type of barking is instinctive and should not be discouraged.

It is only when the barking becomes excessive, and when the excessive barking becomes a bad habit, that the behaviour needs to be modified. Excessive habitual barking, however, is a problem that should be corrected early on. As your Manchester Terrier grows up, you will be able to tell when his barking is purposeful and when it is for no reason. You will become able to distinguish your dog's different barks and their meanings. For example, the bark when someone comes to the door will be different from the bark when he is excited to see you. It is similar to a person's tone of voice, except that the dog has to rely totally on tone of voice because he does not have the benefit of using words. An incessant barker will be evident at an early age.

There are some things that encourage a dog to bark. For example, if your dog barks non-stop for a few minutes and you give him a treat to quieten him, he believes that you are rewarding him for barking. He will associate barking with getting a treat, and will keep doing it until he is rewarded.

FOOD STEALING

Is your dog devising ways of stealing food from your coffee table or cupboard? If so, you must answer the following questions: Is your Manchester Terrier peckish, or is he 'constantly famished' like many dogs seem to be? Face it, some dogs are more food-motivated than others. They are totally

BEGGING

Just like food stealing, begging is a favourite pastime of peckish puppies! It achieves that same lovely result—*food!* Dogs quickly learn that their owners keep the 'good food' for ourselves, and that we humans do not dine on dried food alone. Begging is a conditioned response related to a specific stimulus, time and place. The sounds of the kitchen, tins and bottles opening, crinkling bags, the smell of food in preparation, etc., will excite the dog and soon the paws are in the air!

Here is the solution to stopping this behaviour: Never give in to a beggar! You are rewarding the dog for sitting pretty, jumping up, whining and rubbing his nose into you by giving him food. By ignoring the dog, you will (eventually) force the behaviour into extinction. Note that the behaviour is likely to get worse before it disappears, so be sure there are not any 'softies' in the family who will give in to little 'Oliver' every time he whimpers, 'More, please.'

SEPARATION ANXIETY

Your Manchester Terrier may howl, whine or otherwise vocalise his displeasure at your leaving the house and his being left alone. This is a normal reaction, no different from the child who cries as his mother leaves him on the first day at school. In fact, constant attention can lead to

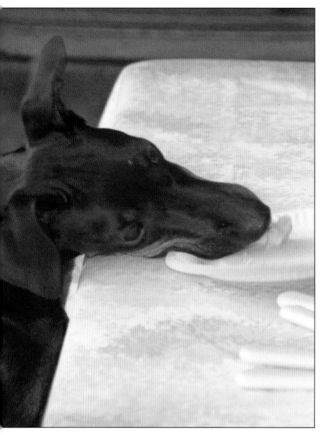

A naughty Manchester having his way with a scrap of food left on the table. Don't lead your Manchester into temptation. Never leave food where your dog can sample it.

obsessed by the smell of food and can only think of their next meal. Food stealing is terrific fun and always yields a great reward—*food*, glorious food.

The owner's goal, therefore, is to be sensible about where food is placed in the home, and to reprimand your dog whenever he is caught in the act of stealing. If the problem persists, place your Manchester in his crate or out in the garden whenever you are preparing food or serving a meal.

separation anxiety in the first place. If you are constantly making a fuss of your dog, he will come to expect this from you all of the time and it will be more traumatic for him when you are not there. Obviously, you enjoy spending time with your dog, and he thrives on your love and attention. However, it should not become a dependent relationship where he is heartbroken without you.

One thing you can do to minimise separation anxiety is to make your entrances and exits as low-key as possible. Do not give your dog a long drawn-out goodbye, and do not lavish him with hugs and kisses when you return. This is giving in to the attention that he craves, and it will only make him miss it more when you are away. Another thing you can try is to give your dog a treat when you leave; this will not only keep him occupied and keep his mind off the fact that you have just left, but it will also help him associate your leaving with a pleasant experience.

You may have to accustom your dog to being left alone at intervals. Of course, when your dog starts whimpering as you approach the door, your first instinct will be to run to him and comfort him, but do not do it! Eventually he will adjust to your absence. His anxiety stems from being placed in an unfamiliar situation; by familiarising him with being alone, he will learn that he will survive. That is not to say you should purposely leave your dog home alone, but the dog needs to know that, while he can depend on you for his care, you do not have to be by his side 24 hours a day.

When the dog is alone in the house, he should be confined to his designated dog-proof area of the house. This should be the area in which he sleeps and already feels comfortable so he will feel more at ease when he is alone.

COPROPHAGIA

Faeces eating is, to humans, one of the most disgusting behaviours that their dog could engage in, yet to the dog it is perfectly normal. It

Pining by the window sill, this Manchester is awaiting his master's return home.

Manchester Terriers are excellent watchdogs and will stand guard by your gates. Having a canine chum in the garden makes a long day without his master much more tolerable.

is hard for us to understand why a dog would want to eat his own faeces. He could be seeking certain nutrients that are missing from his diet, he could be just plain peckish or he could be attracted by the pleasing (to a dog) scent. While coprophagia most often refers to the dog eating his own faeces, a dog may just as likely eat that of another animal as well if he comes across it. Dogs often find the stool of cats and horses more palatable than that of other dogs. Vets have found that diets with a low

AGE OF ANXIETY
The number of dogs that suffer from separation anxiety is on the rise as more and more pet owners find themselves at work all day. New attention is being paid to this problem, which is especially hard to diagnose since it is only evident when the dog is alone. Research is currently being done to help educate dog owners about separation anxiety and how they can help minimise this problem in their dogs.

digestibility, containing relatively low levels of fibre and high levels of starch, increase coprophagia. Therefore, high-fibre diets may decrease the likelihood of dogs' eating faeces. Both the consistency of the stool (how firm it feels in the dog's mouth) and the presence of undigested nutrients increase the likelihood. Once the dog develops diarrhoea from faeces eating, it will likely stop this distasteful habit.

To discourage this behaviour, first make sure that the food you are feeding your dog is nutritionally complete and that he is getting enough of it. If changes in his diet do not seem to work, and no medical cause can be found, you will have to modify the behaviour through environmental controls before it becomes a habit. The best way to prevent your dog from eating his stool is to make it unavailable—clean up after he eliminates and remove any stool from the garden. If it is not there, he cannot eat it.

Reprimanding for stool eating rarely impresses the dog. Vets recommend distracting the dog while he is in the act of stool eating. Coprophagia is seen most frequently in pups 6 to 12 months of age, and usually disappears around the dog's first birthday.

Discuss coprophagia with your vet. The best way to prevent this problematic behaviour is to keep the garden clean by poop-scooping every day.

INDEX

My Manchester Terrier

Dog's Name _____

Date _____ Photographer _____